SOLDIER IN THE WEST

THE CIVIL WAR LETTERS OF
Alfred Lacey Hough

SOLDIER IN THE WEST

* * * * * * * * * *

PHILADELPHIA

THE CIVIL WAR LETTERS OF
Alfred Lacey Hough

* * * * * * * * *

edited by
ROBERT G. ATHEARN

with an Introduction by
JOHN NEWBOLD HOUGH

UNIVERSITY OF PENNSYLVANIA PRESS

© 1957 by the Trustees of the University of Pennsylvania
Published in Great Britain, India, and Pakistan
by the Oxford University Press
London, Bombay, and Karachi

Library of Congress Catalogue Card Number 56-13432

Printed in the United States of America

To JOHN NEWBOLD HOUGH

Whose Respect for History

Helped to Preserve This Bit of

the American Civil War

EDITOR'S PREFACE

* * * * * * * * *

THE CIVIL WAR letters of Alfred Lacey Hough furnish the historian of that period with sufficient supplementary evidence fully to justify their reproduction for his use. This thirty-five-year-old commission merchant, who entered the war as a sergeant of Pennsylvania Volunteers and came out of the conflict as a Brevet Lieutenant Colonel, saw more than the shot-and-shell side of the struggle. Although he preferred to be in the field, he was placed on occasional recruiting assignments, he served as Commissary of Musters for the Army of the Cumberland, and in addition to this variance of duty he was attached to the staff of General James S. Negley and later that of General George H. Thomas. It is from these different assignments that the reader will vicariously experience the several sides of military life, including the exciting and the routine.

Captain Hough—the actual rank he carried during most of the war—was in complete earnest with regard to the war aims, from both a personal and national standpoint, and as a result he took extreme care to preserve for his descendants all of his experiences and observations in the great crusade of his time. Although his letters carry the normal questions and

7

answers concerning family life and friends at home, they seem to impart an unusually good picture of life in camp as well as the position of the individual with reference to the larger military scene. His comments on various important officers with whom he had contact are of interest and may possibly contribute something for future biographers of these men.

Looking at his letters as a whole, the reader is left with several general impressions which are worthy of consideration. First, he will get some of the feeling of a man who entered the conflict for purely patriotic reasons and who stressed the "hell-begotten conspiracy" theme from the first letter to the last. He will also gain some idea of conditions on the home front from Hough's constant admonitions to his wife to be patient, to try to complain less about the difficulties of inflationary living, and to stay with him on the moral question involved in the great conflict. The picture of a volunteer militia officer emerging as a professional soldier will also become apparent before the reading of the letters has been completed. In this respect Hough was typical of thousands upon thousands of civilians who threw themselves into the war hoping to be of assistance but usually completely untrained for that which was to follow. By the end of the war the writer was an old campaigner and, more than that, he had decided that army life was the only life. He had become the general's senior aide at the conclusion of the war and remained at his side until Thomas died in 1870.

The present work is derived from the following sources:

1. A typescript of Capt. Hough's letters to his wife, made from the originals about 1909 under the supervision of his son, Judge Charles M. Hough, and

now in the possession of his grandson, John N. Hough. Some of the originals, which he deemed too personal, were destroyed by Capt. Hough himself before his death and are therefore not available. The whole collection of originals was destroyed after the typescript was made.

2. A manuscript "Autobiography" which Hough began in 1875 and maintained concurrently with his military service until his retirement in 1890. This manuscript is also in the possession of his grandson. It was composed from letters to his wife, official data in his possession, and brief memoranda made occasionally. The manuscript consists of 245 legal-size pages, of which pages 1-73 deal with the period of his military service to the date of the surrender of General Lee.

Supplementary material is drawn from time to time, whenever it sheds further light upon the text of the two above, from four other sources:

a. The typescript of the letters from Capt. Hough's wife to him. These were typed and the originals destroyed as were those of Captain Hough.

b. Marginal notes in the typescript of his father's letters made by and in the handwriting of Judge Charles M. Hough. These stem from long personal association with his father and conversations with him during Judge Hough's adult years.

c. Comments drawn from Judge Hough's Memoirs, an unpublished typescript in the possession of his son, composed at various intervals between 1918 and 1924.

d. Sundry papers and letters relative to the Hough and Merrill families, note of which will be made upon citation. These are used chiefly as source material for the biographical essay immediately following, but occasionally provide illumination also for the text of the letters and autobiography.

Because of the destruction of the original letters it has been impossible to check their wording, spelling, and punctuation. The editor, however, has every reason to believe that the typing was done with reasonable care and accuracy; certainly no glaring errors or incomprehensible passages exist, but the quotation of certain letters in the Autobiography affords an opportunity to compare the typescript with what Major Hough "copied" from the letters at a time when they were still in his possession. Such a comparison shows certain discrepancies in wording and punctuation, but in not a single case is the meaning of the text altered.

The handwriting of the Autobiography, although on the whole very legible, occasionally causes some difficulty. Evidently such difficulty was at times encountered by the typist of the typescript for in the entire body of letters there are some half-dozen spaces left blank for a word which seemed illegible. Some of these words are filled in, in the handwriting of Judge Charles M. Hough; others are still blank. In one instance such a blank occurs in a letter quoted in the Autobiography and can thus be supplied from this source. On some few occasions the typist also made what appear to be genuine misinterpretations of the handwriting.

In the matter of wording, it would appear that when writing the Autobiography Major Hough fairly frequently permitted himself to copy phrases which, perhaps unconsciously, reshaped themselves in his mind as he wrote. Familiarity with the content of his own letters as well as any of many well-recognized practices of copyists will account for all such variations, and not one of them affects in any way the meaning of the whole. Examples: the change from *commenced* to *began* (twice) and the omissions of an officer's title in one letter; the change from "on we went, none of us knowing our destination" (typescript) to "on we went, not knowing our destination" (Autobiography). Many others could be given, and since such differences seem in general to be those characteristic of a copyist familiar with his own work rather than of a typist dealing with unfamiliar work, it is reasonable to assume that the typescript represents what was originally written more accurately than Hough's subsequent quotations. In any case it is the text of the typescript that is given, and the content is identical.

In the matter of punctuation the two sources differ even more widely. The typescript is normally punctuated, and sentences properly ended at reasonable intervals. The Autobiography, however, was written with very little regard to schoolbook principles, and the disentangling of sentences is occasionally made the harder by the difficulty of distinguishing between large and small letters. The writer rarely employs any mark of punctuation other than commas, and furthermore strings whole sentences, independently constructed, into a series separated only by commas. The resultant effect may run as long as eight or ten lines of manuscript. Moreover in some cases where a capital letter clearly marks the inception of a new sentence, the preceding symbol actually looks more like a comma than a period. In other cases, regardless of the symbol used, the first letter of what should be a new sentence is frequently so formed as to leave considerable doubt whether it is large or small. This very marked characteristic of Hough's handwriting, though having no bearing on the meaning of his words, is so disturbing to the modern reader that the editor has thought best to repunctuate passages taken from the autobiography in more accord with modern principles.

Some nineteenth-century spellings (e.g., battallion) are consistently employed in the Autobiography and have been faithfully preserved by the typist of the letters. Also unchanged are certain Briticisms (shewed) and general misspellings, all of which have been reproduced as they appear both in the letters and autobiography. The first occurrence only is marked by an editorial [sic].

Sections omitted from the letters are marked by a series of dots. These sections are, without exception, entirely concerned with family matters and have been omitted solely in the interests of conservation of space and preservation of the interest of the reader. Nothing has been omitted which in any way conflicts with what is presented, there is no effort or intent to edit out anything which would change or even supplement the picture of the war or the life of the soldier. Messages to friends, inquiries concerning friends and relations, further expressions of endearment to his wife and children constitute the burden of the excised passages, which if printed would neither embarrass the writer's descendants nor add to the interest of the letters. In instances where entire letters have been wholly omitted, comment and explanation are offered in the text.

Acknowledgment for financial assistance rendered is given to the Council on Research and Creative Writing of the University of Colorado. Thanks for advice and suggestions go to Professors Avery Craven and Colin B. Goodykoontz. The editor's particular acknowledgment is tendered to Professor John N. Hough, Uni-

versity of Colorado, who preferred not to accept any
of the editorial responsibility in presenting his grand-
father's letters for fear of reflecting family prejudice,
but who did a good deal of the routine checking and
unpleasant proofreading.

ROBERT G. ATHEARN

University of Colorado

ILLUSTRATIONS

(The illustrations appear as a group following page 128)

Alfred Lacey Hough, 1853

Alfred and Mary Hough

Alfred Lacey Hough, 1861

General James S. Negley

General William S. Rosecrans

General George H. Thomas

Retreat of the Confederates from Corinth

Ruins of Atlanta

Lee and Gordon's Mills, Chickamauga battlefield

[The illustrations appear as a group following page ...]

INTRODUCTION

* * * * * * * * *

ALFRED LACEY HOUGH was in the late fifties representative of what many men were before him, and fewer after, the modern American, emerging from a shell of Neo-Colonial isolation which had encased his forebears in the relative provincialism of southern New Jersey landed gentry. His abandonment of this type of life, not entirely by choice, had great influence on the formation of his opinions, as did also the connections he made by marriage outside the normal range of his fathers'. The coincidence of these two events with the commencement of what he always referred to as the War of the Rebellion, created the Alfred Hough who was to experience the spiritual development that many of his more restless American predecessors on the eastern coast had known decades before him. They also created the man who, by virtue of this differentiation from his own forebears, was the direct stimulus to the more active and broadened life that has characterized his descendants. For these reasons a brief sketch of his own background and the influences at work upon his character in his formative years is a valuable aid to any interpretation of his letters of the Civil War period or even of his own autobiographical record.

Early in the 1680's, within a year and a half of Penn's arrival in this country, there came from Macclesfield, England, one Richard Hough, "yeoman," and Thomas Hough, his indentured apprentice. Thomas (whether younger brother or nephew is not known, and Richard quickly disappears from the records) settled some twenty odd miles east of town, in Burlington County, New Jersey, where he became the progenitor of a family, moderately numerous as families went in those days, of "farmers" who in four generations had established sufficient local respect to lend their name to the hamlet neighboring their farms, Houghtown. They were as typical a country gentry as could be re-established on this side of the Atlantic Ocean, landholding gentlemen who built solid houses and had "good" furniture, whose fields were tilled by hands other than their own, and who did not "work" after three o'clock in the afternoon, a fact into which some of their descendants have thought it best not to inquire too closely. With no pretensions to learning or to political influence, the line was vigorous and "respectable," increasingly rigid, even if Thomas was not originally a believing Quaker. Having maintained a neutrality excused by religious convictions during the Revolutionary War, their life was relatively stable until the changes of the early nineteenth century forced upon them the same fate, only partially foreseen by Alfred Hough's father, as that of the English country squire a few generations earlier.

Unheralded, the changing fortunes of the Houghs began with the appearance in the family of Alfred's mother. She was a second wife but, more important, a Lacey. The Laceys were originally from Bucks County, Pennsylvania, and had stemmed from John Lacey (Brigadier General in the Revolution, a not very distin-

guished soldier but highly useful in the Valley Forge
district because he knew it well from boyhood) and his
wife, an Irish Reynolds, of post-Quaker immigration
into the Burlington County area. Their daughter, Jane
Chapman Lacey, in the home of the retired General at
Pemberton, New Jersey, moved in an aura of lofty intellectual pretensions high above the Hough tradition
(poetry was composed in the house!), but was not
above accepting the hand of the lately widowed but not
inconsolable Jonathan Hough. This was the first weakening in the Quaker armor of the Houghs, and was not
improbably partly responsible for the discontent which
Jonathan began to show with the limited life of a country gentleman. With some but not enough foresight of
the iron age approaching (but not foreseeing the importance of coal), he sank the family wealth in a char-
coal-producing enterprise whose proportions extended
beyond his resources. Involved with him in bankruptcy
was his wife's brother (as well as the instigator of the
plan, Jerome Bonaparte), and while he was in the com-
plicated midst of efforts to recoup he died, insolvent,
in 1829.

Jane Hough was left with five living children, none
over twelve; Alfred Lacey, the next to youngest, born
April 23, 1826, being then three years of age. Her
Lacey brother indulged his sorrow in social escapades
which the Hough family thought it better to forget.
And thus Alfred's mother was left a widow, poorer
than any Hough or Lacey tradition would envisage,
living in the shadow of various Hough relatives whose
opinion of Jonathan's attempts to make money was
exceeded only by their contempt and lack of sympathy
with anyone who had been so unwise as to die insolvent.
Withdrawal to a more modest house in the village

(which also reflected the downfall of the family fortune by changing its name to Juliustown after a prominent local weaver) did not heal the troubled heart of Jane, and by 1840 she moved inconspicuously to Philadelphia where she lived humbly with her children. As soon as they could work or the daughters were old enough to marry, she was dependent upon them.

Thus one hundred and fifty years of land-mindedness and family clannishness had not prepared either mother or children for the city bourgeoisie life which was now theirs to live. Dutiful but uncongenial visits to maiden aunts in Juliustown and more happy times with better situated Newbold cousins in the same area, kept the bond from wholly breaking. John, the elder brother, clung to it more tenaciously, as is reflected in all his later life, but Alfred grew up with a new restlessness born of city associations, a greatly weakened Quakerdom, and a Lacey tradition of military rather than landed respectability.

One of his forebears, a great-great-uncle, was reputed to have studied medicine, but an early death was visited upon him for this sin of heterodoxy. An older brother actually pulled up stakes and emigrated to Iowa, a fact which may perhaps have opened Alfred's eyes to possibilities beyond the New Jersey horizon. But cholera had taken him before he was fairly settled, and the clannishness of the family is proved by the fact that he is the only male of Hough name (to this day) not buried in the family plot at the Friends Meeting House near Juliustown. The two older sisters had initiated the break in tradition by marrying, one an engineer of German extraction who came with the first railroad to Juliustown, another a fairly prominent Philadelphia doctor, but both were soon widowed. The

engineer, as if to point up the changed situation in the
family, had been a "paying guest" in the Houghs'
modest home in Juliustown before the move to Philadelphia, and the son of this marriage, the oldest grand-
child, became a wholesale grocer in the city. Thus did
the break begin in Alfred's generation.

John, the elder brother, also entered the wholesale
grocery business, married, and went back to the Quaker
fold, even stricter than before, and ever desirous of
recovering the family lands. Alfred and his mother
moved to a new and cheap section of town (north of
Market Street), which meant no social pretensions. A
year or two at an "Academy" and frequent visits to the
Newbolds and to Uncle Darlington (William Darlington, the noted botanist, husband of Jane Lacey Hough's
sister) exposed Alfred to a more liberal and intellectual
atmosphere than ever would have befallen him even if
more favorable circumstance had attended his father's
charcoal speculations. Such was his education, molded
largely by Laceys and Darlingtons and by acquaintance
with a library which no Jersey Hough would have had.
Day by day he was won over to the ways of the city.

Alfred began as a clerk in Parrish's Apothecary
shop, intending to become a dispensing chemist, but a
kindly Providence had given him a too fine sense of
smell which the chemicals displeased; he hated clerking
and had now a good excuse to change. Again with a
Parrish, he became a commission agent for a paper
manufacturing house and eventually won the position of
a partner. Tempted somewhat by the lure of the Mexi-
can War, whether from patriotism or opportunity cannot now be said, he was detained by maternal tears. His
leisure time was turned rather to the allurements of
city life, a Schuylkill boating society, some political

clubs (Whig), dining and theaters; before he was thirty
he became, in a modest way, something of a man about
town. More important for his later career, he joined
the Washington Grays, a home militia organization
with social pretensions and gay uniforms. An end to
Quakerdom could not be more finely foreshadowed.
Handsome in his uniform, and possibly a political asset
for Harrisburg, he found himself appointed a "Colonel" on the staff of Governor Pollock. Among the not
so arduous duties of this "office" was attendance upon
the Governor at some official function in Harrisburg
where he met a Miss Mary Jane Merrill, whose ante-
cedents and background were not only very different
from his but were destined strongly to influence the ex-
Quaker who still retained a serious and somber temperament. Scarcely had he married Miss Merrill when
the crash of 1857 wiped out Parrish & Hough, if not as
thoroughly as Jonathan had been, at least enough to
send Alfred into another living connected with a Mr.
Jackson, then a well-known lumber, coal, and iron
speculator, from which no more than a modest income
was obtainable. Unspectacularly the new family, increased shortly by two sons, Charles and Lacey, lived
together with the still inconsolable and irreconciled
Jane Lacey Hough. Her death in the same year left
Alfred now entirely free of Hough and Lacey tradi-
tions, and ready for the new influence of the Merrills.

Mary Jane Merrill was a singularly attractive
young woman, full of joy and even a little inclined to
the frivolous, enjoying in the prosperous home of her
father in New Berlin, Pennsylvania, a social position
untrammeled by serious financial considerations, and
without doubt the object of attention from more than
one eligible young bachelor. But this was only the out-

ward appearance. When she had met "Col." Hough at
the Governor's reception she was already a young
woman of twenty-five who had known deep sorrow and
had experienced bitterness in her home. Her father,
James Merrill, a very prominent and highly respected
lawyer, had died when she was only nineteen, her
mother long before, leaving two children: Mary Jane
three years old, and Charles one year. She had had two
stepmothers since then, neither one congenial to her,
though not actually hostile. Her own brother Charles,
whom she adored in the image of her departed father,
exhibited certain weaknesses which she took it upon herself to restrict and if possible to reform, while simul-
taneously she became fearful lest he influence her
younger half brothers in the same direction. She had
been engaged before, but her fiancé had died. If this
were not enough, the strong Calvinistic indoctrination
which James Merrill had brought with him from the
original Merrill home in northern Vermont left her
with no uncertain theological belief in predestined
damnation. The vitality of her natural temperament
struggled with this fierce religion in the breast of this
alert and charming woman. If the former seemed to
win it was but a shallow victory, marked by a week-day
façade of cheer, severely divorced from the Scotch
Presbyterian dogmatism of the Sabbath. Such was the
paradoxical nature that loved and married the serious
and somber ex-Quaker who had probably never once
struggled with the inner emotions of love and God that
had so clouded the life of Mary Merrill.

If this marriage was a pairing of unlike souls, it
could never be questioned that the companionship was
deep and enduring. If Alfred Hough was constitution-
ally unable to understand his wife's religious ante-

cedents or penetrate the ratiocinations of her mind, she
was equally incapable of sharing what seemed to her a
sobriety of attitude without an explicable religious or
personal raison d'être. To him she undoubtedly con-
tributed confirmation of his sense of duty and conscience inherited perforce from Quakerdom, while to
her he clearly brought such love and freedom as she
would permit her conscience to remake into the pleasant
surroundings of a youth she had really never known.
The opposites of their true natures were blended by
the compelling forces of their circumstances: she, the
essentially charming and gay young woman who could
not free herself from a sad and strict background, and
he the somber young Quaker who had only recently
known the freedom of the city bachelor.

The interaction of the two natures apparently
fused them into a solid front, for in 1861 two widely
different circumstances forced decisions which would
seriously affect their future. The first was the death of
the last of the maiden aunts at Juliustown, the last of
his father's generation, and with it the opportunity to
inherit the old position in the country. There was no
real question. The old distaste was never truly obliter-
ated, and there were no regrets at the final severance
from the New Jersey connection. His elder brother
John, never so sharply separated and now revived in
his Quakerdom by his recent marriage, played the
family part in this and henceforth, though maintaining
his home and business still in Philadelphia, it was he,
not Alfred, who was the Hough of Juliustown.

The other circumstance was the war. This he accepted of his own choice, confirmed and strengthened
by his wife, who shared the sense of honor and service
that he exhibited in his volunteering. Never, though the

years were long and the separation hard, did either of them waver in the firm conviction that he was doing the right thing, by his country and his, or her, God. The dependence on her confirmation of his judgment, seen repeatedly in his letters whenever an important decision affecting them both had to be made, is perhaps evidence of his recognition that her decision might be arrived at by a different chain of thought from his, but the agreement between the two, though he was far from young by military standards (thirty-five), married, and had two children, was absolute and final. If hardship had to be endured, it was no new experience to her, and to him a sacred duty. Typically, his brother John, now forty-one and excusable on religious grounds, did not go.

The sense of satisfaction with which the soldier did his duty, even when distasteful or when seeming to promise no promotion, needs no comment beyond his letters themselves. That his wife played her part to the utmost is equally apparent from hers. No public urging such as we have recently experienced, could have produced any more domestically detailed epistles than hers; quotations of long conversation of the children, details of friends and home, chitchat and local gossip, patiently retold in full, as well as serious discussions, questions, and expressions of opinion on the state of the war and of the Union, all gave to the absent Captain the only substitute for the companionship he had won, and lost. One of the finest tributes to Mrs. Hough's cheer and spirit is the comment of Captain Hough's clerk quoted by him in a letter. If a letter can reveal her character through her husband's facial expression while reading it, she had done a magnificent job indeed.

"Crazy Hough" they called him on Market Street, for he had long prophesied the war as the only means of settling the slavery question. This appellation he won from his business associates, especially the "Constitutional dry goods" men, who sold goods to the South and voted for Bell and Everett in 1860. But such was his conviction, and now he embraced it as the fulfillment of his prophecy, the proof of his sanity, and the opportunity, if one were further needed, to leave Burlington County and even Philadelphia behind spiritually as well as physically. The end of Quakerdom and of the country squire had come.

His convictions concerning the war during his service are clear enough from his letters. There is no change in the spirit, well-nigh that of a Crusader, which he constantly exhibits. As strong language as he ever uses is bestowed upon the iniquity of the "hell-begotten conspiracy" of the South, and as violent anger as he ever permitted himself to show is unleashed against the $300 draft dodgers in Pennsylvania. He fervently wishes that his two sons were old enough to serve their country too, and he feels that the issue of the war will determine for generations whether he and his children are to live in anarchy or in happy homes. His faith never wavered, even in the disappointment of failing to achieve promotion, or in the gloom of the financial outlook. Once, and only once, toward the end, he began to wonder if he might not owe it to his family to provide a better living by retirement from the Army because the government simply was not providing for its servants in uniform and the thought of the bounties infuriated him. But he did not retire, and the belief in the principles if not in the rewards of what he was fighting for did not change. Rewards would be won in the satisfaction of service faithfully done, and for the lonely hard-hit family left at home the rewards would be those which Providence grants to the faithful and the long-suffering. Such beliefs could not be either strange or meaningless to the ex-Quaker Captain or to his Calvinistic wife.

Yet with the war's end they alone would hardly have been enough to tip the balance in favor of remaining permanently in the Army. Another, and as it turned out a lifelong, influence had developed during the latter years of the war. Chance had thrown the Captain into an association with General George H. Thomas, and before the end of the war he was serving on his staff. Though this association was slow to develop, as shown by his repeated efforts after Chickamauga to obtain a different position and to remain with General Negley, the affection for "Pop" Thomas gradually became the dominant force in Captain Hough's life and certainly in his military career. This was no exception to the power which General Thomas had to attract and retain the devoted loyalty of men. When the opportunity came to return to civil life, though strong attractions were offered by his former business associates in the paper industry, the prospect of remaining in the official family of the man he loved and admired as "a model soldier" was an even stronger force. That it meant never recovering the financial independence or the social position which Mary Merrill had given up in New Berlin and which they might have achieved together by a return to civil life in Philadelphia, must have been the subject of many long evening conversations in Nashville, after his family had joined him in the spring of '65; but no record of them is available save the comment penned ten years later: "Although I have not repented of my decision, for I have been happy in the service, I must confess that had I foreseen that the army would be reduced, and my promotion so long delayed, I should have decided otherwise." Thus did he pay for the unexplained disappearance of his name from the Commission list in 1861, and its restoration only by political influence of Simon Cameron and at the end of the order of promotion.

The subsequent life of Captain Hough was that of any Officer in the American West of the seventies and eighties. Remaining with General Thomas till the latter's death in 1870, he saw service from Nashville to Alaska. Thereafter at various posts in the Indian West, in Texas, and in New York harbor, his military service typifies the Army career of those years. Letters (extant from various periods during which he was absent from his wife) and the autobiographical record which he began in 1875 and kept current till his retirement, show ever broadening experience of military and national affairs. He was widely acquainted among military men and had a considerable correspondence, especially in connection with the various controversies which raged around the memory of General Thomas, both concerning the battle of Nashville and his alleged refusal of a commission in the Confederate Army. From his notes at the time is taken the account of General Thomas' death at San Francisco in Thomas B. Van Horne's *The Life of General George H. Thomas,* Charles Scribner's Sons, 1882. The publication of this book gave (then) Lt. Col. Hough great satisfaction in the manner of presentation of the General's character and military ability.

Colonel Hough was retired in 1890, after twenty-nine years of service in the United States Army. Four

years later his wife died, after which he made his home
first with his son, then a lawyer in New York, and later
with his daughter, Mrs. W. R. Hall, in Princeton, New
Jersey. The death of his brother John in 1896 left him
the sole survivor of his generation, and having the good
fortune to live well past the maturity of his own two
surviving children, he found in them the companionship
he had lost in the death of his wife. It is to the intimacy
with his son, now U. S. Judge Charles Merrill Hough,
o'erleaping the barrier of years and filial relationship,
to which Judge Hough's knowledge of his father's character and experiences was owed. Life in the frontier
posts where his father had been stationed had begotten
the usual boyhood impressions, but the association of
maturer years gave the Judge a much clearer insight
into the mélange of circumstances which had produced
the relative simplicity of the Hough tradition and the
complexity of the Merrill, and between them developed
the character and personality of Colonel Hough.

In 1908 the veteran of army life died. He was
then a Brigadier General (Retired) although he never
used the rank, which had been conferred in 1904. It is
therefore not upon personal acquaintance that this account of his life is based, but upon conversation with
my father, Judge Hough, before his death in 1927, with
his sister, Mrs. W. R. Hall, who lived until 1946, and
from the memoirs which Judge Hough composed concerning the family background and his own life.

JOHN NEWBOLD HOUGH
University of Colorado

SOLDIER IN THE WEST

THE CIVIL WAR LETTERS OF
Alfred Lacey Hough

1

* * * * * * * * *

On the tenth day of January, 1875, the commanding officer of Fort Brady, Michigan, sat down and commenced a task which he had long put off. Major Alfred Lacey Hough, 22nd United States Infantry, now began to write his memoirs and commenced by saying, "As part of my life has been somewhat eventful, and some of my experiences novel to the many, I have thought a brief narrative of important incidents would be interesting to my children, more especially those relating to the War of the Rebellion; that great historical period."

After looking back over the events of those busy years he decided that 1860 was his logical point of departure, and he began to write. "The election of Abraham Lincoln to the Presidency of the United States was the direct cause of wonderful and marked changes in the lives of millions of people, and among them my own. In 1860 I was leading a quiet uneventful life in Philadelphia, Pa., doing a mercantile business as a Commission Agent of Manufacturers of paper. Soon after the election it was evident to me that a great struggle was about to take place between the Government and the Southern States, and it [omission?] on record among my comrades that I believed war not improbable. I was at that time an Honorary member of the 'Artillery Corps of Washington Grays' one of the leading companies of Volunteer Militia of Philadelphia, having served my seven years as *active* service in the corps to entitle me to Honorary membership. Believing war was possible and if it occurred my company would offer its services, I went again on the active list and made all arrangements to cast my lot with it. When, after the fall of Sumpter [*sic*], the call for troops came, I was prepared and ready to go. As I had anticipated, the Company did offer its services and was accepted, and I was mustered into the U.S. Service as a sergeant of one of the companies ('F') of which the Washington Grays made two of the 17th Regiment Penna. Vols., Colonel Frank Patterson comdg."

After a careful explanation of his ardent patriotic feelings and his belief in an adherence to the wishes of the majority of the electorate, as balanced off against his personal reluctance to leave his family, the writer described the departure of the Washington Grays for war.

"On the 8th day of May 1861 our regiment left Philadelphia for the south, we had in our ranks the very flower of the youth of Phila; there were but few men of my age, the great majority were just at manhood, and from the solid families of the City. We marched to the Baltimore R R Depot through a mass of our friends and relatives who cheered us on while their tears could not be held back. I will mention here that all but one man of our Regiment returned in safety from this expedition, but not finally from the war. I cannot speak for others than the two Washington Gray

Companies A & F but of these more than three fourths subsequently served as officers in the war and a large number of these fell before the enemy or by disease.

"We arrived in Washington about 2 A.M. on the 10th but as this journey was my first experience in the war, and it being a remarkable one from the fact that our command comprised the first troops that passed through Baltimore after the citizens of that place had attacked passing troops and blocked the way for them [?], I will give a detailed account from my first letter from Washington."

It was not in his first, but his second letter from the nation's capital that Hough related his experiences in Baltimore and began his series of home letters which he continued faithfully until the end of the conflict when he could be with his family again. His initial letter, typical of men away from home, simply states that he has arrived safely at his destination.

> Capitol of the United States
> House of Representatives
> Washington City, May 9, 1861
> Camp Cadwalader

My Dear Wife:

On my own authority I suppose you will think you have a right to be worried now, as I told you you need not be while we remained here. But my own dear wife you must not be, although we move from here tomorrow. Where to I do not know, but we are to move. We have orders within the last hour to have everything packed and ready. The Quarter-Master is packing up the stores and our baggage wagons are on the way to Camp. From the preparations, in my military judgment

we are going some distance, and, as we carry everything we are not going into any immediate action. So
my Dearest I have no doubt the papers will inform you
of our movements, and you will know where we are
before any demonstration will be made. I do not think
however we will move South. Genl [George] Cadwalader is here, and I think we will be attached to his
command, and be in service either in Maryland or Virginia. But this is all conjecture as we have no positive
information, neither have our officers. In fact we have
not been *told* we are to move, only to be ready. But *I*
know it from a confidential source. As soon as this letter
is finished I shall proceed to pack up and get a good
night's rest, which I shall need, as I was on guard last
night. I am very well my dearest and feel prepared to
undergo the necessary fatigue of a march. I feel very
thankful to a kind Providence for his protection so far,
and have an abiding faith that his will with me is right.
You know my dearest that this service is with me a
conscientious duty, and I am perfectly willing and prepared to meet its responsibilities. So far we have been
more than favored, having had a very pleasant Camp,
the best and most comfortable no doubt of any now in
the field. As we have but a short time more to serve,
and we are in good health, and good discipline, it is
right that we should bear a portion of the labor that
our less favored brethren have been performing. You
need expect no more letters from this Camp, but as
soon as we get to another post I will write at once. If
in the meantime you learn from the papers our destination please write me *at once* directing the same as before, only changing the name of the place. . . . your

Affectionate Husband,

Alfred

11 A.M. Washington May 10 1861

My dear Wife:

I have sent you two short despatches, and now will write you a letter if I am not called off for duty before finishing, which is very likely as we are waiting orders.

To commence: We came off from home in fine condition as the papers will have informed you, such enthusiasm, and such a crowd I never saw, tinged with sadness however, by many tears shed by the loving and loved ones left behind us. We arrived safely at Perryville, and for the first time I felt I was really a soldier. We found it a garrisoned camp, with sentinels, tents, huts, &c. &c. We were quartered in the depot, and had just lain down on the floor to sleep when we [were?] ordered to pack up and mount, where to we knew not. It was a short mount however, only on board a steamer at the wharf. We again laid down on rather *harder* boards than in the depot. Imagine a large barn floor entirely covered with humanity fully clothed, rolled up in blankets, with a knapsack for a pillow; such we were, I mean our company; the other companies were quartered in the same way in other boats or out-buildings excepting one which could find no place, so laid upon the ground surrounding a large fire. I did not sleep very well, but got enough for rest. We were roused at daylight by the drum, answered roll call, and performed our ablutions in the river. The scene was delightful at sunrise, a bright beautiful morning, with beautiful scenery surrounding. After roll call we betook ourselves to our haversacks, all I believe with gracious appetites. I did my duty I know. I here want to acknowledge the worth of the "eggs", and "cold tea" both were delightful; they added to good ham sandwiches of which I had plenty I have lived on so far; hot coffee has been dealt

out frequently but I have stuck to tea. After "grub" the
rest of the troops embarked, bag and baggage, the
whole command consisted of our regiment 780 men,
Maj. Sherman's battery [1] of 8 pieces about 100 men
and 60 horses and 5 companies of infantry from Texas,
the latter about the hardest looking party I ever saw
having seen rough service on the frontier, they had but
5 officers left, the rest all having joined the—Rebels,
so we understood. Our whole command occupied 5
steamers. We got under way about 11 A.M. with colors
flying, and drums beating; the sail down the bay, all the
steamers filled and all close together was glorious. On
we went none of us knowing our destination.

Before we left the Armory we were provided with 10
rounds of cartridge each, and 3 days' rations. Nothing
more was done that indicated our movements till we
rounded the Patuxent light, when we headed in for Baltimore then we knew our destination. We were then put
in line, and every man given *15 more* rounds of cartridge; this looked like work. We landed at the railroad
wharf amid the cheers of the crews of several U. S.
vessels, answered well back by us; just before landing
the Colonel gave an order loud enough to be heard by
all the vessels, and the people on shore. "If attacked
fire by platoons." At once we could see people start off
from amidst the crowd on shore, to spread the news as
we supposed. I then turned my thoughts upon myself,
offered up a prayer for myself and my dear ones, then
to my work. I can say, my dearest, I did not feel the
least emotion of fear, and believe I could have gone
through almost anything. But minnie muskets and ball
cartridge have done the work. We did not meet with the

1 Thomas West Sherman. He became a lieutenant colonel, Fifth
Artillery, on 14 May 1861.

least trouble, everything was peaceable, but no cheering from the people, but occasionally an *individual* congratulated us upon our arrival. We marched up the bank and were placed in Northern cars, and now our discomfort commenced; after waiting an hour we were told that sufficient cars had not been provided, and we must get out and march to the Camden Depot 3 miles. We did so leaving those cars for the regulars and the baggage; so the whole regiment formed and made the march by ourselves through Baltimore, without the least molestation. When we got to the depot we were still short of cars, and had to crowd in awfully. We landed at Baltimore at 6 o'clock and did not get off till 9. at the Camden Depot the crowd was immense and decidedly Union, the few Rebels among them were silenced. We were much congratulated upon our coming by many solid people in the crowd. Finally the other trains came up with the regulars, making three in all, we in the van, and we were off for Washington which we reached at 1 A.M. this morning, cheered all along the line by the troops guarding the road. It was a most tedious ride; we got into quarters at 2; a large vacant hall opposite the National [Hotel]. We had a soft plank again for a bed, and I slept soundly. We are now waiting orders, and receiving the congratulations of Pennsylvanians for our march. I am *very well*. My own dear wife remember me in your prayers till we meet again which I feel will be surely. Much love to all, and write at once; if we leave here a letter will follow me. Kiss the little ones.

Alfred

I must not omit to state that a squad of police were about all the time, seeming to be the strongest Union people, but the citizens said they were not at heart.

In Camp at Washington, D. C.
May 13th, 1861

My own dear wife:

. . . Soon after writing last we were ordered to quarter in the Senate Chamber. We had very good sleeping quarters on the carpeted floors, but the *dining rooms* were horrible, down in the vaults. We staid there till yesterday morning when we packed up and marched to this Camp, about 3 miles; it was a pretty hard march, loaded as we were, and the sun terribly hot. We are well quartered now, in a beautiful retired spot, and I slept soundly last night in our tent. We get fresh meat to-day for the first time; it will go good but I cannot complain of my appetite; I eat first rate but I have had to come to coffee, it seems like meat and drink both for me. I hope it won't disagree with me; if it does I will quit. We have made a decided sensation in Washington. We were applauded as we marched down Pennsylvania Avenue, and the people say we compare favorably with any regiment yet on the ground. We have pretty arduous guard duty here, being on the extreme outpost here, a secession Camp is within 3 miles of us. They are prowling around us all the time, and we captured one this morning who came within our lines with a Sharps rifle in his hand. We see very few white folks around our Camp, but the free negroes around all the time with refreshments to sell; it is quite a harvest for them. I am very well, as well as the whole regiment, excepting a few slight ailings, and our duty has been very severe so far, everything being new yet to us. . . . We have not yet named the Camp, when we have I will advise you.

Alfred

Address

Sergt. Alfred L. Hough,
Company F
Col. [Frank E.] Patterson's Regiment,
1st Pa. Volunteers,
Washington, D. C.

Camp Cadwalader, May 22/61

Dearest Mary:

I have yours of yesterday and welcome it is, for a more homelike interesting letter I never had. Your history of the children's little doings is very grateful to me, and the descriptions of the sewing party at the Church made me laugh heartily. You speak of my "notes". My dearest you must not expect long letters from me. I really have not time to write, the only time I have from duty is from dinner, say 1½ or 2 till 4 P.M. and you must know how little we feel like writing then after a hard morning's work commencing at sunrise, and just finished at that. I will write you often but short, in fact I have nothing to write about. It is the same thing every day over and over again. . . . I still keep well, was threatened with a bilious attack yesterday but took some medicine at once, and to-day am fine again. You must not be worried at what the papers say, when we are in action it is time enough. But what did we come here for my dear if not to fight? You ask me how often I am on guard all night; about once a week. My turn will come tomorrow again.

Oh there is one thing in your letter that needs explanation. You say you hope the eatables and *"drinkables"* were sent, pray what of the latter were sent? The peaches were splendid and so was the *juice;* perhaps it was that you mean, or was it the tea? I wish you would send me some of my good brandy; I can get nothing but whiskey here when I want stimulus and that don't suit me. Don't be afraid, I wont abuse it, and it would do me good some times. . . .

Alfred

Camp Cadwalader, Sunday,
May 26/61

My Own Dear Wife:

I have not heard from you since my last, but suppose there is a letter on the way. Lacey [2] will have told you all the exciting news about affairs here. Since he left nothing new has occurred, although there was a great excitement in Washington yesterday, troops were moving, &c. caused by a false alarm that the Secessionists had attacked our troops over the river. The report was groundless, caused by a bonfire and the target practice of our troops. We have been in readiness to march for two days, but there is no excitement in Camp, everything goes on as quietly as if we were at home attending to business. In Washington and Georgetown all is excitement, but with us it is the reverse. How soon we become accustomed to War, it seems as if I had been a soldier for years. Night before last news came to the Camp that the Jersey troops had taken a battery of 9 guns at the point of the bayonet without firing a gun, losing 43 men. We gave 3 cheers for them, talked about it for a few minutes, expressed our disappointment at not having had the same chance, and all was quiet again. This news was false of course. Yesterday during the false alarm in Washington orders came out to take our arms and await orders to march; we were ready in 5 minutes, waited anxiously for an hour or so and received countermanding orders; in an hour it was forgot-

[2] Lacey Goddard, a nephew.

ten. To-day we are going through our regular routine
as if nothing had happened; it seems strange when I
think how short a time we have been here, that we
should be in such a condition. The only time I have felt
any real excitement was the night the troops crossed
over the river. I was Sergeant of the Guard and dis-
tinctly heard the tramp although 2 or more miles off.
I reported to the officer of the day who called the
Colonel, he came out and listened for a while, and returned to his tent; in a few minutes I saw a number of
men coming quietly out of their tents; they formed
and marched out of Camp 40 in all picked men. I was
relieved from guard and went; we left so quietly that
the rest of the Camp knew nothing of it. The Colonel
marched us around the country, through Georgetown,
crossing all the roads leading to the river, but could find
nothing; got back to Camp near morning, and retired
without waking up the list. It was a bright beautiful
moonlight night, and our tramp was really exciting. The
next morning the cause of the noise was explained and
then again we were disappointed that we had not been
sent. We have got now into regular Camp life, and are
more comfortable every day. We have somebody from
Philadelphia here every day, so we hear constantly from
home. The ladies are beginning to come now to see their
friends, and this morning I heard a child cry in the
Camp. Oh! how I did think of my little ones. It does
seem like a long time yet before I can see you, but it is
so good to hear that you are comfortably situated and
all well. The accounts we get from Philadelphia of mercantile and financial matters are very gloomy. I hope
they will change some time, or there must be great distress there. I should think however that the manufacturers ought to be busy. This War ought to make some
kinds of business good. . . . I don't know anything

about our future movements, in fact we get all the news
here through the Press and New York papers.

Your Husband

Poolesville, Md.,
Saturday evening

My Own Dear Wife:

We have just arrived at this place, and the mail
leaves at one so can only write a few words. There are
only 2 mails a week. We are now 35 miles from Washington, on our way to Harpers Ferry. We have advanced on the enemy and they have fled, without giving
us a chance at them. There was a body of them here
yesterday but they left last night, our next point is a
9 gun Battery across the Potomac about 10 miles. We
shall ford the river and take it if they don't run away,
which we are led to believe they will, as they have run
so far. The people here are for the Union, as they have
been mostly along the route, but they have been over-
awed by the Secessionists till we came among them.[3]
I am very well, but it was very hot marching to-day.
Love to all, Good-bye,

Alfred

We are about 3 miles from the Potomac.

In Bivouack at Rockville, Md.
Tuesday 11th June 10 A.M.

My Own Dear Wife:

As I wrote you we left Camp yesterday morning at
11. We marched 11 miles yesterday and 8 this morning;

[3] "The people in this immediate region are for the Government
almost to a man. Those at Rockville are reported to me as being about
one-half rabid secessionists, calling themselves 'States-rights' men."
Report of Colonel Charles P. Stone, June 11, 1861, Headquarters of
Rockville Expedition, *Official Records*, Series I, Vol. II, 106.

it has been a pretty hard march on a/c of the heat, but we have all come in in good condition. We stopped yesterday through the heat of the afternoon and at night bivouacked in a field, for the first time we slept in the open air, and I slept delightfully. Was very tired of course, and could have slept on flints. We started at 7 this morning and made the march of 8 miles by 10½ o'clock. Considering that we carried our heavy knapsacks, 2 days rations, 25 rounds of cartridge, our guns, &c., and it being very hot, and a hilly country, our march was a very good one. We have joined here 2 other Regiments of infantry, a company of Dragoons and Sherman's Battery who came a day before us. And while I am writing, another Regiment is in sight to be followed by others, all to concentrate here under the command of Col. [Charles P.] Stone. How long we shall stay here, and where we are going I know not. But we shall not stay long here, as we are not pitching our tents. I know you are anxious about me and I take the first opportunity of writing. I am very well, and as soon as I get some dinner I shall stretch out and rest myself on the ground. I must say I am astonished at the way I stand this hard work; I never was better in my life than I am now. We have met with nothing astonishing so far, the country being thinly settled, but at this little place, with so many troops here all is excitement. The people are generally for the Union, but there are some Secessionists among them. A troop of Secession Cavalry left here yesterday on our approach. I have no doubt our destination is to let off some ammunition at Harpers Ferry but I *know* nothing. I am writing on my knee and cooking dinner at the same time, and am so much interrupted that I must close in time for mail. Write to me at once at *Washington* as the letters will be sent after

us. Much love to all my dearest, Good-bye for the
present.

Alfred

Rockville, Md., June 13th 1861

My Dearest Wife:

We are still here in the same position as when I last
wrote, ready to march at any moment, everything
packed but our blankets and cooking utensils, with nothing to do but cook, eat and sleep, which latter we do on
the ground in the open air still. Although I personally
have a great deal to do, as I have charge of all the
cooking for our Company, I having been found to be
the most fit man after several others having their turn,
that is I am the *head cook* and superintend the squad
only, but it keeps me very busy. We find we are in a
hotbed of secession. The people with a few exceptions
are against us; they are only cowed. We have great
difficulty in getting vegetables, the people generally are
afraid to sell them to us. But the longer we are here the
better we get along, as we strengthen the Union sentiment, and our friends lose their timidity. I was very
fortunate in getting a negro woman to hire our company her kitchen and stove for baking (as we draw
flour now) so we have fresh bread and cakes, but some
of the other Companies have to do their own baking,
and such bread! So yesterday after several failures,
some of them went to the only bakery in town, who had
previously refused to bake for them, and took orders
from the Colonel that he *must* bake or have his bakery
taken possession of; he "caved" at once. I recite this to
show the feeling here. There was no American flag
waving when we arrived but now there are several. We
are still in the dark as to our destination. We suppose

it is towards Harpers Ferry but do not know. We are all very well, and have astonished our Colonel with our ability to stand the fatigue of marching. I have become satisfied of one thing, that is, cultivated men get along better under privations than the "roughs". Our Companies, and the Philadelphia Grays grumbled less and stood it better during the mount than the others, and we live better on the same food than they do; we are careful and managing and they are shiftless. It grieved me very much to leave all the good things behind at Camp Cadwalader, but we had to do it. . . . I wish you could see our bivouack, it is very picturesque. We are in a grove of woods by the roadside on the outskirt of the village, a large field of grass back of us, which leaves the view open on both sides. The muskets stacked with the accoutrements hanging on them, the men sitting and lying on their knapsacks, in all kinds of positions, it is the reality of many pictures I have seen. Our baggage train and horses are drawn up on one side, you can imagine it. I did not expect to have the pleasure of writing to you from here again, and do not think I can do so again, but will write every opportunity I have.

Alfred

Poolesville, June 18/61

My Dearest Wife:

. . . We are now realizing the real life of a soldier, in an out of the way place, living on rations, sleeping on the ground, hard drilling and hard work every day, and being within sight of the enemy have constant guard duty, and sleep on our arms every night. Our camp ground here is a miserable place, an old work-out tobacco field, where hogs have been running and rooting, so that we are in the midst of dust, and if we had rain it would be mud. We of course cannot keep clean. It is an important position however and must be held till more important demonstrations are made. I will endeavor to give you a plan of our position. We are in the centre of half of a circle made by a bend of the Potomac about 3 miles from the river with 4 or more roads leading to ferries or fords, all of which are occupied on the Virginian side by the enemy, and were on this side till we came. They have all the boats on their side and the river is too high now to ford, which accounts for our not moving forward. We are 15 miles in a direct line from Harpers Ferry, and 25 by the river. We are encamped by ourselves with a battery of 2 guns and 2 companies of dragoons, the New Hampshire regiment is 2 miles above us and the N. York 2 miles below; there are more of our troops in the neighborhood, but how many I do not know. We have a detachment placed on the bank of the river to watch the enemy. Yesterday morning during drill we heard the firing of cannon on the river. We were under arms in a few minutes ready for moving; how the boys did jump at the prospect of a scrimmage, but we were doomed to disappointment; it was the rascals on the other side firing across the river at our detachment to amuse themselves of course; they came down to the bank and haled for us to come over, using the most vile language. If we only could get across we would stop their mouths quick enough; and since their amusement of yesterday we have taken a different course; last night 25 picked men, sharp shooters, were sent down to the river to pink them off if they attempted the same game, and as we hear a musket shot occasionally we suppose they are doing it. We hear but not officially that Harpers Ferry is evacuated; if so I fear we shall not have an opportunity of distinguishing ourselves, as our time will expire before the Government will be ready to make a demonstration into Virginia I think, although we may force a passage across the river if the water falls sufficient to ford. This was a great point for them to get supplies, all of which we have stopped. It bothers me to make out this population. The secessionists have left, many of them being in the Army in Virginia. The rest of the population appear loyal, but indifferent, excepting some who are delighted to see us and say this is the first time they have felt safe since the trouble. They complain terribly of the secessionists, charging them with all sorts of crimes, &c., &c. I have come to the conclusion that the honest old farmers are strongly for the Union, the Lawyers and rich planters are for secession, and the rabble go with the party in power. We have had no demonstration of a secession feeling other than indifference, but have had great feeling shown in many instances on the Union side; on several occasions on our march old farmers' wives came down to the roadside to cheer us on, crying God bless you *gentlemen;* God bless you boys, Our flag forever, &c., &c. How this would bring tears to our eyes. On one occasion I could hardly contain myself; at the outskirts of a village through which we passed, a lady had brought her little boy, about like our Charlie, to the roadside and seated him on the gate post; in his hand he held an American flag, which he waved at her command, she saying God Bless you. How our boys cheered; but I could not; I thought of you and the children and rushed from the ranks and kissed the dear boy, wetting his face with my tears. Since we have been here several old farmers have brought us bread and cakes to give us, thanking us for coming; so you see we are strengthening the Union feeling; and so it will be till the end, but the secessionists must be crushed, nothing else will do for them; they will never make good citizens again. We were much amused on Sunday with the darkies. They congregated around the camp to see us, and such a motley dressed crowd I never saw before. Our negro Methodists could have taken patterns from them. You know I never look at ladies' dresses, but I took a good look at some of the black damsels. I had a good laugh at their finery. I believe I have told you all that would interest in this monotonous place, for it is emphatically a *one-horse* town. To show you how primitive some of the people are, the women ride around our camp two of them on *one horse*. . . .

God bless you and yours.

Alfred

2

*   *   *   *   *   *   *   *   *

WHILE Sergeant Hough was amusing himself at Poolesville by writing letters home that described the garb of the colored ladies, the relative degree of loyalty among the citizens, and one-horse qualities of the town, events were happening in Washington which were to change his entire life. As he described it in his Autobiography, some of his friends of influence had made application for his appointment as Captain in the Regular Army and their efforts had been successful. Hough's subsequent description of the business of getting a commission was much more complete than what he had to say in his letters home to his wife.

"I arrived in Washington on the 25th day of June and proceeded in accordance with the advice I had received to the Adjutant General of the Army, Col. Lorenzo Thomas, and reported myself to accept the position of Captain in the U. S. Army. I was in Sergeants uniform, somewhat shabby from wear; the Colonel was polite but rather austere in his manner, as he looked at me as though I was an impostor, and told me there was no such an appointment made. I was annoyed, of course, and hurried out to my friend, the Hon. Wm. D. Kelley M. C. [Representative from Pennsylvania]

who advised me of my appointment. Upon finding him,
he was as much astonished as myself, he said the Sect.
of War Genl. [Simon] Cameron had told him that I
was appointed, and returned with me to the Adjutant
General and asked him if he was not mistaken. The
books were looked over and the same reply was made,
'no such name on the books.' My friend then arranged
for me to meet the Sect. of War personally that evening
at Willards Hotel which I did. He expressed himself as
much astonished that I was not appointed, as he dis-
tinctly recollected sending my name in for appointment.
He closed the interview by handing me his card and telling me to present that the next morning at 10 o'clock at
his private office. The next mornings experience I shall
never forget. Promptly at 10 o'clock I presented myself
in the corridor of the War Dept. before the door leading to the Secretarys office. I was in sergeants uniform,
both it and myself being rather the worse for wear, at
least in appearance. Around me were some twenty or
thirty officers brilliant in their new uniforms, with gilt
and brass resplendent, all waiting for the Sect. of War,
the negro looked at me from head to foot and answered
severely, as if I, a common soldier could have no business with so great a man. 'The Secretary is engaged
you can't see him.' I took out the card, handed it to him,
and told him to give that to the Secretary; he took it,
looked at it, then looked at me, closed the door and dis-
appeared. In a few moments he returned, opened the
door, peered among the crowd till he saw me, and in the
most humble and polite manner exclaimed, 'Captain,
the Secretary says wait here and he will be out in a
moment.' I shall never forget the looks of the surrounding officers, heretofore they had been inclined to look
upon me as an intruder, now I was an object of curios-

ity. In a few moments the door opened and General
Cameron came out accompanied by a gentleman whom
I afterwards learned to be Senator Phelps of Vt. The
General looked around, recognized me, came up to me,
took my arm saying 'Come along with me' and we three
marched into the Adjutant Generals office, leaving the
officers dancing attendance on the front of the door. A
few moments in the Adjutant Generals room accomplished the business. Genl Cameron told Col. Thomas
I had been appointed some days before. The Col. said
he had never received the notice, the General said it was
very strange and aided the matter by directing my appointment to be made out at once, and in a few minutes
I left the War Dept. with my appointment as Captain
19th Infty in my pocket. This was on the 29th day of
June 1861."

That same day—the 29th—the newly appointed
captain wrote home, telling his wife of his change of
status. His letter expresses concern over his future
domestic situation, rather than any elaboration of details on his recent promotion.

Washington, D. C., June 29, 1861
My Dearest Wife:
At the last moment I expected to be here I received
my appointment of Captain in 19th Regt of Infantry
with orders to report in person at headquarters. Indianapolis. It of course stopped my going to camp at once.
I reflected upon it last night, and finally concluded to
accept it, which I did to-day. I have now to go back to
Poolesville where I shall be detained a few days. I shall
then get home as fast as possible where I hope to be by
Saturday next at farthest. I shall then get ready and go
to Indianapolis to report. If I find I shall be there any

time I will want you and the children to go with me, but that I must decide when I see you. Shall we keep our house? Or what shall we do? Think about this so that we can fix matters with despatch. You need not write to Poolesville but please drop me a line here at Willards [Hotel] so that I can get it on my way home. . . . Affectionately your husband,

Alfred L. Hough,
Captain 19th Infantry,
U. S. A.

Indianapolis, July 16 .61

My Dear Wife:

. . . Our blanks &c. arrived from Washington to-day so I suppose I shall get off to Terre Haute in a few days. I tried hard to get my station changed to this place but could not.

I fear we shall have a hard time to get recruits from all accounts; the people will volunteer but not join the regular army. I shall look for boarding for a "family" as soon as I get there. Everybody says it is a very pleasant place. Do you know anybody there? I am getting along famously in a military way. We have examinations in tactics, and regulations, and practice in tactics for three hours every day; the latter has been conducted by Capt. Nilson, the old Ohio Captain I spoke of. He went home on leave to-day and Colonel appointed me instructor during his absence, and I have performed my duties to-day with satisfaction to myself. So I feel rather proud to be drilling Captains and Lieutenants, most of whom have been officers before. The balance of the time I am occupied in preparing myself for such examinations as the Colonel gives us, I have no time from business except evenings. I am very well but feel pretty tired to-night, now 10 o'clock, so I think I will go to bed, and if I have anything more to say will do it in the morning. So good night, God bless you, dearest.

Alfred

*   *   *   *   *   *   *   *

3

* * * * * * * * *

Hough's LETTER HOME, on July 16, was the last one written until April of the following year. After reporting for duty at Indianapolis he moved on to Terre Haute where he was placed on recruiting duty. His family now joined him and the occasion for letter writing ceased. "My life at Terre Haute was tiresome," the newly commissioned officer wrote, "and I longed to be in the field. I interested myself however by organizing a Home Guard, the Union Rifles, composed of the young businessmen of the place, these I instructed and was the means of preparing a number of young men for Officers of Volunteers which they subsequently became." During April, 1862, orders were issued which placed Hough in command of Company F, 1st Battalion, 19th Infantry. This particular command was of a temporary nature since a Captain Mulligan, then on detached service, was the actual commander of the group. Hough's company was yet to be organized. On April 22, Company F, Captain Hough commanding, left Indianapolis aboard the transport *B. Q. Adams* and after a river trip of five days, arrived at Pittsburg Landing, three weeks after the bitter battle of Shiloh. His war letters are resumed with a brief note written aboard the south-bound transport on April 24, 1862.

On Board Transport B. Q. Adams,
50 Miles below Louisville,
Apl. 24th, 1862, 8 A.M.

My Dearest Wife:

I wrote you from Louisville last night saying we should get off to-day, but we got off last night and expect to be at Pittsburg Landing on Sunday night. We are all well and in good condition so far. I have about 200 men and 6 officers besides my own company all under my command with directions to report to Genl. Halleck.[1] I am very busy of course. Shall write again the first opportunity; in the meantime you write and direct to Capt. A. L. Hough, 19th U. S. Infty Rousseaus Brigade,[2] McCook's[3] Division, Army of the Ohio, and leave it with Col. [Edward A.] King, who will forward it first opportunity. . . .

Alfred

On Board Transport B. Q. Adams,
Apl 26th 1862 2 P.M.

My Dearest Mary:

We are now about 100 miles from Pittsburg Landing and all safe and in good condition. (The boat shakes so I cannot write). This is the first leisure moment I have had from active business, but am now all prepared to leave and march as soon as I report. We shall be there in the night and I shall report tomorrow. The regiment is some 10 miles from the landing and I expect to be with it on Monday night. . . . I have to re-

[1] Major General Henry W. Halleck, commanding the Department of the Mississippi.

[2] Brigadier General Lovell H. Rousseau, commanding the Fourth Brigade, Army of the Ohio.

[3] Brigadier General Alexander McDowell McCook, United States Army, commanding the Second Division, Army of the Ohio.

port to Headquarters and get rid of my extra command
and get transportation for my own. I have been thankful that I have been so busy and felt such a responsibility for it has kept me occupied, and made me feel that
I am doing something by serving my country that war-
rants me in making such a sacrifice of personal feeling as I do in leaving all that is dear to me in this
world. . . .

My men have behaved well and I have good assistance in Mr. [Lt. Howard E.] Stansbury; I have them
organized for comfort, have selected two good cooks
(old sailors), and the boys are delighted with their new
captain. They say they have not had such good *grub*
since they have enlisted. They are well now, but I came
very near losing one of them. They will drink (some of
them) if they can get liquor; I have kept a strong watch
to prevent any coming aboard, but in spite of me some
was smuggled aboard by newsboys and apple boys in
small vials; one of them at Evansville [Indiana] sold
one of my men a vial of something that he drank, and
in 15 minutes he was seized with most violent illness
with every symptom of poison. I was sent for and my
medical knowledge was called into service. I have great
assistance also in Mr. Stansbury, who is quite a doctor.
We vomited him; he was also purged violently; then
had cramps, and was cold, very near death. We then
put hot applications and brought him to. We nursed
him faithfully till we came to Mt. Vernon [Indiana]
some hours after in the night, sent for a doctor who said
the man had been poisoned with something very like
arsenic, and that we had treated him perfectly correct,
and he would be well in a day or two. I had him brought
upstairs and put on my cot, he is now going about and
tomorrow will be well. It has one good effect; I am not

afraid of the men drinking any more smuggled liquor. We get a doctor on board at Paducah so I feel better satisfied. . . . I have no other incident that would interest you; we hear no news and do not know what is going on in the world; we are not crowded and are very comfortable in the boat, she is very fast and we pass everything which makes some excitement. This is a beautiful river, and to-day is a beautiful day, and after finishing this I am going on deck to enjoy for the first time for 10 days a little leisure. Troops are coming here from all directions. . . .

Your faithful and affectionate husband

Alfred

On Board B. Q. Adams,
Pittsburg Landing,
Monday Apl 28th 1862

My Dearest Wife:

It would take me hours to tell you all my adventures during the last 36 hours. I cannot do it in this letter but will make a short abstract of it. Arrived at Pittsburg Landing Saturday night at 8 o'clock, went ashore, waded through mud to Halleck's quarters [?] 3 miles got orders and back again about 10. Boat went to upper Landing, 2 miles, went ashore next morning at 5, and through mud again to Buell's [4] quarters, then McCook's, then Maj. [omitted] about 4 miles, got a horse and back to boat. Water had risen so much could not land troops, and use new lock to Pittsburg Landing, will be off in about an hour, and march to camp will be there before night. *All well.* . . .

Alfred

[4] Major General Don Carlos Buell, United States Army, commanding the Army of the Ohio.

Camp Rattlesnake,
About 8 miles from Pittsburg
Landing, April 30th 10 P.M.

My Own Dear Wife:

I snatch a few moments from the active business I have constantly had since leaving you to write, this being the first opportunity since landing that I could get a letter to the Landing. . . . In the first place I am *very well* and *very* comfortable; have a good tent and writing on a good desk, and have a good fire before my tent. To commence where I left off in my last. I landed my Company and marched them to headquarters. Pitched tents and was immediately ordered out to drill with the regiment—then supper and to bed, and next morning break up camp and marched to this place near the line between Tennessee and Mississippi, I don't know which State it is in. We have troops all around us, and in good condition; you need have no fear of a surprise. Buell's army is in splendid condition. I know nothing of Grant's as I have not seen it. He is not in favor here however. We had to march without our baggage which came up to-day. We had to huddle together last night but are very comfortable now, have been drilling all day. All my writing is behind, which will take me several days to bring up. I have no assistance, as Mr. Stansbury has been detached and made Quarter Master; so you see I am busy indeed. You have no idea how much work is required to make a new company comfortable; but I have done it to theirs and Maj. [Stephen D.] Carpenter's satisfaction. As a whole I am much pleased with my company; they behave well; I have some sick but none seriously ill. Every man that I left Indianapolis with was mustered to-day, which was a great gratification to me. I think we will be in this camp four days more. We moved forward yesterday, and a division moves every day; there are four more divisions to move; we are lapping one another every day slowly and easily. We were in the front yesterday but to-day another division is in front of us. Our officers are inclined to think there will be no battle, but we poor underlings know nothing about it. We are now encamped in a very pretty place in the woods on a high ridge near a clear little brook and everything looks fresh and green not yet destroyed by a camp; but the road out here from the landing is terrible to contemplate. For miles you cannot travel without seeing either far or near the results of the great battle of Shiloh; [5] here are the remains of horses, burned to prevent their decay; there the ashes of burned camps and here again rows of graves—some more carefully made than others, with little wooden head boards with the name in pencil work. But the reality is soon accustomed to. I have nothing like the shock in looking at it that I would have in walking through one of our old cemeteries that hold the remains of my old friends, and it is astonishing how callous the men become. I was really amused yesterday on the march listening to the conversation of the men; just as we passed a grave one was talking about his land warrant, another pointing to the grave said, "There's some feller's got his already", which was received as a pleasant sally. Such is our life here. . . . Major Carpenter has won laurels with everybody. What a gallant man he is. He is so sick that he can scarcely hold up his head but goes through with all his work, with conscientious industry; he is a lesson for anybody; I am proud to be serving under such a man. I have told you all about our camp, and that is all I

[5] Fought on April 6 and 7.

know; we have rumors every day of what has happened
—one is that New Orleans is taken, and another that
Yorktown is taken; but we don't believe anything, and
get no papers at all.[6] . . . God bless you and preserve
you and my dear children is the prayer of your Husband,

Alfred

In Camp Near Corinth [7]
May 16th or 17th 1862

My Dearest Wife:

. . . We have not moved since my last letter, nor do
I see any immediate prospect of moving immediately.
Since being in this Camp we have done nothing out of
the ordinary course of camp (and drill) life excepting
a reconnaisance [sic] in force yesterday. We marched
out of camp prepared for a fight if necessary, went about
2 miles halted, sat down to rest, remained about 3 hours,
and then marched home again. Such was our "reconnaisance in force". It is all explained in this way. We
are the reserve Division as I told you in my last, the
reconnaisance was made by another Division, and one
Brigade was selected as the reserve for that Division,
so while we were sitting still, they were making the reconnaisance expected of us. If they had been attacked and
forced back we would have "gone in" and finished the
work, but as we heard no firing, we suppose they found
nothing. I understand they were within 3 miles of Corinth. I predict that if the rebels stand the battle will
be an artillery one. They will not come out of the entrenchments but will remain and be cannonaded out. My

---

[6] New Orleans was in Union hands by April 29. Yorktown was
taken May 4.

[7] Corinth, Mississippi, twenty-two miles south of Pittsburg Landing.

position in the fight will be this: McCook's Division having established its reputation in the last battle has been selected as the reserve, to be brought up when all else fails. As I do not think there will be any failure, we will have but little to do. I do not know what troops are in our division excepting our own brigade, but our brigade is a splendid one; we have the 15th, 16th and 19th regulars, 1st Ohio commanded by Capt. (now Vol. Col.) [Benjamin F.] Smith a regular and old friend of mine . . . 6th Indiana, 15th Ohio, and the Louisville Legion,[8] Rousseau's old regiment, and Capt. [William R.] Terrell's regular battery, as good a one as is in the service—all commanded by Genl. Rousseau, as gallant a soldier and accomplished a gentleman [9] as I ever met; he is a great favorite with all of our officers, our old regular officers such as Maj. Carpenter think the world of him. I cannot say as much of McCook although a regular; he is only a Capt. in the regular service, but a Brig. Genl. of Vol. He is a good fighting man, but coarse, without dignity. He is much set up with his elevation and is overbearing to his officers although many are his superiors in rank in the regular service. We have however confidence in him in battle. Our Brigade consists of the very first troops that went into Kentucky so you see they have had large experience. We have a reputation, and are expected to keep it and are therefore in the reserve for the final stroke. When I arrived the Major was much exercised at the prospect of having a green Company in the battle then daily expected; con-

8 Fifth Kentucky Infantry.

9 More than eight years after writing this judgment, Alfred Lacey Hough made the following note on this letter with regard to Rousseau. "Changed my mind about this. A.L.H." Near the notation is another, in the handwriting of his son, Charles M. Hough, which says, "This is the only comment made by my father on any of these letters."

sequently I was kept hard at work drilling them in which I took a deal of pride as I was determined to win his confidence. He told me yesterday that he saw a *very great improvement in* my company and was not at all afraid to trust me when necessary and wound up by telling me that when Capt. Mulligan arrived which is expected soon that I would be assigned to other duty, and I need not expect to be relieved during this campaign. . . . We have hard work to live here, can get nothing but army rations, except fresh bread occasionally; have had no butter for a week, but it is wholesome. The worst of it is the tea that we get is very poor, and I miss our old tea so much. I cannot imagine what our dignitaries are doing that we should lie here to long, but have no doubt it is all right.[10] This is their last stronghold, and I suppose we are making sure of destroying them. So must it be.

. . . Give my love to all of the household. (I note what you say of Col. [Edward A.] King; from what I can hear of him here I think you formed a correct opinion of him; he is not popular here). . . .

Yr Husband

Alfred

In Camp near Corinth,
May 22nd, 1862

My Own Dear Wife:

. . . We are still in the old camp undergoing the usual routine, nothing new to tell; hear cannonading for a few minutes every day, get ready to march, noise ceases, and we go on with our drill &c. To-day it is as

[10] Halleck had started for Corinth on April 29 and spent the whole month of May covering the fifteen mile distance from the Shiloh battlefield to the approaches to Corinth. Stanley F. Horn, *The Army of Tennessee, A Military History,* New York, 1941, 148.

quiet as New Berlin here, and a beautiful summer day. I am still very well as are the most of our troops. There is a little fever but few deaths. The first one in our regiment for a long time occurred last night, the one in my company that I spoke of. The poor fellow died last night suddenly; I just reached him in time. I had him buried this morning and have now a detail protecting his grave building a fence around it placing head board, &c. I have just finished writing to his father in Crawford Co., Penn.; it has been a melancholy morning for me. I have all the requisite papers to make out &c. which will keep me busy to-day. . . . I am getting out of the way of business now and wish I had something to read for recreation, but nothing is to be had here. In fact there is nothing in this country, either to eat, to wear, to read, or anything else *but to drill.* We get a paper once in a while about two weeks old and that is all; we are so far from the landing that we have but little communication with the world. We are not allowed to go out of the Division lines and consequently cannot get to the front to know what is going. We have a great many rumors every day after we hear firing, but we *know nothing.* I however have put all the information I can get together and believe I can give you a pretty good idea of how our army stands by the following diagram. I have no map to draw it from, the proportions will therefore not be correct.

You will see from that every corps d'armée is within supporting distance of each other. The attack will be made it is said as follows: the centre and left of Buell's army, and centre and left of Thomas' army will make the attack with artillery a large quantity of which they are now placing. If they are unsuccessful and are driven back (which is almost impossible) Pope's army on the

left, the right of Thomas' army and our Division go in
to their assistance and hold our position. If they are
successful and the rebels attempt to retreat while the
main army pursues them, Pope will move to the left and
cut off the Memphis R[ail]Road, the eastern road is
already cut off. If they, the rebels, should see that they
are caged and attempt to make a detour to the west and
come in our rear, McClernand's reserve will prevent
that. This I believe is the plan and is all the war news
I can give, and this is not *positive*. . . . believe me ever
your Husband

                                                Alfred

                              May 29th or 30th 1862
                              Before Corinth

Dearest Mary:

We have fought the great fight, and "nobody hurt".
We left camp last Tuesday morning, have had skirmishing, &c., been under fire at long range, heard bullets
whistle past, &c., but without having a real battle, were
just ready to pounce in on them to-day, when we found
the bird had flown. They kept up a splendid show of
force, and must have completely outgeneraled us,—although among us subalterns the belief was current that
we should find no enemy, but our Generals thought or
at least acted differently. We were about a ½ mile from
their fortifications. I understand our cavalry and some
artillery are pursuing but it wont amount to anything.[11]
To tell the truth there is a feeling of "big disgust" at
the whole thing; we feel as if we had undergone privations that would have justified our destroying their

[11] A brigade of Pope's cavalry was sent in pursuit and managed to
destroy a trainload of ammunition and supplies at Booneville. Stanley
F. Horn, *The Army of Tennessee*, 152.

army instead of letting it run away; but perhaps we may do it yet. I have not seen anybody that has been in Corinth but understand a body of our troops are there, whether we shall go on or back to Camp I know not all is uncertain. I am not very well, have the diarrhoea badly, but not ill; I always tell you exactly how I am. The doctor says I will be well in a few days. . . . God be praised for relieving you of one fear. I have gone through the *Battle* of Corinth. The loss of our whole Brigade is 13 wounded, 1 mortally, only 2 in our Battallion.

Yr Husband

Alfred

May 31st 1862

My dearest Wife:

. . . I wrote yesterday saying Corinth was evacuated, and that I was not very well. I am glad you will get this sooner as I am now all right again and shall take command of my company tomorrow again. To tell the whole story, diarrhoea commenced on me last Sunday, and by Tuesday had run me down considerably, when we were ordered to march at once. As I knew it must be to fight, I could not stay behind although I was not well enough to go, so the doctor said. But I felt as if I should be almost as willing to die on the road as to be suspected of cowardice, so went and grew worse as I went. Slept that night on the ground and the next marched into battle as we supposed took possession of a hill with no opposition except what our driving in their pickets amounted to; the whole loss in our Brigade was only 13 wounded, only 2 in our Battalion and none in my company. A few bullets whistled near me and that is all the fight we had. We lay there that night and threw up intrenchments as we knew we were within shelling distance from their works, we began to believe that they had left, although there was heavy firing on our left. That night we had several false alarms and stampede of a team all of which kept me awake. The next morning a Deserter informed us that Corinth was evacuated, and as by that time I was pretty sick and had behaved well all through, I yielded to the Doctor and Major and went to Camp on horseback, went under treatment got rest and with the blessing of God am convalescent and will go on duty tomorrow. Our troops went into Corinth, and to-day are all back in Camp in good condition. To sum up the whole, we have been outgeneralled, and there is a feeling of intense disgust at everybody and everything that leads our Armies.[12] The evacuation was perfect, what they did not take they destroyed. Their works were very fine, and it would have cost us many lives to attack them in front, but that we should not have done, and that they knew, hence their running. Some of our troops are pursuing but with what success I know not. They kept up a show of force by strong picket guards, who suffered very severely by the advance of our lines, we found several dead in front of us, and the fight on our left that I spoke of was very severe on them. Even the last night when they were almost all gone, they had their bands playing at 3 in the morning, calls beating, &c. Didn't they fool us bad? It

[12] General U. S. Grant agreed with this completely. He remarked that "On our side I know officers and men of the Army of the Tennessee—and I presume the same is true of those of the other commands —were disappointed at the result. They could not see how the mere occupation of places was to close the war while large and effective rebel armies existed." Grant was convinced that Confederate morale must have been raised by their ability to remove not only the troops but their supplies as well. U. S. Grant, *Personal Memoirs of U. S. Grant,* New York, 1885, II, 381.

may be all for the best but we can't see it. We want to get out of this country; what we are going to do we have not the least idea, we will know in time I suppose. . . . Love to all.

Alfred

Iuka, Miss.
25 miles east of Corinth
June 12th or 13th

My Dearest Mary:

. . . We are resting here to-day and shall march on towards the East I suppose to Huntsville, Ala. Being on the march we have no writing conveniences and it may be some time before I shall have another opportunity of sending a letter. Our march will be about 150 miles; it will take us some 10 days or two weeks I suppose, but when we get there I shall be much nearer you by mail. But we may not be going there, we do not hear it officially. But we are going east, that is certain and there is no enemy near us here. I had intended writing you a long letter giving a full account of the march on Corinth &c. but circumstances prevented till it is too late now; you must wait till I tell it you. . . .

Yr true husband,

Alfred

In Camp 1 mile below Florence, Ala.
South Bank of Tenn. River,
June 16th, 1862

My Own Dear Wife:

. . . I have gone through a great deal in the last three weeks, much more in the way of deprivation of the comforts of life, and severe taxation of my powers of endurance than I ever experienced before. . . . So much has occurred, and so long a time has elapsed since my last descriptive letter, that I may not be able to give you a full account of my experience but will try. Some time during the 4th week in May I was seized with a diarrhoea, which almost everybody had in our old camp between Pittsburg and Corinth. It did not trouble me at first but by Sunday the 25th it became so bad and I felt so miserable that I concluded to rest, and went off duty. I remained in my tent taking medicine but kept about statu-quo till Tuesday night, when orders were issued to be ready to march to the front at 6 o'clock next morning prepared for battle. This order was a heavy blow to me. I feared my inability to go through with it, sleeping on the ground, no chance to cook, in fact everything to do but what a sick man should do. But how could I stay behind? This the first battle, and the very one I was sent here to help fight! How could my absence be explained to my friends (or enemies if I have any). All this I weighed well, and finally felt that I must go. Major Carpenter said I had better not go, and the Doctor refused to put me on duty. But I made ready for the start and in the morning moved with them. But to save myself as much as possible rode in the ambulance. We reached our entrenchments and stopped for the night,— next morning I was no better, but still able to push on. This day we expected to fight so I took my place at the head of my company. About 10 o'clock in the morning we moved, crossed our entrenchments and marched to the right and front about two miles. We were now on disputed ground, the night before it had been occupied by both Picket Guards whose firing had been heard by us continually. We reached the foot of a hill in a dense forest which covers the whole country here. Here we were halted, and word given along the line, not to speak a word, but move along in silence, and be prepared to obey any order at a moment's warning. (When I speak of *we* I mean our Brigade which when in line of battle would reach about a third of a mile, no other part of our Division can be seen by us). Our first order was "Forward into line", which was soon executed. The next, "Right shoulder shift arms", which indicated readiness for anything. At this time I felt as cool and collected as ever I did in my life and for the time was as strong. I felt a great work was in my hands and I must execute it. I had 50 men who looked to me for their every action, and almost for their every thought. I knew they had confidence in me, and if I did my duty they would do theirs. If we moved a step farther we should go where none of our army had been before, so waited anxiously for the next order. A line of skirmishers were thrown in front of us, and then the order was heard very lowly given, "Forward March". Forward we went, quietly, solidly, and firmly. Not a sound was heard excepting the cracking of the bushes beneath our feet, we could just see our skirmishers occasionally, about 50 yards in front of us but no further. Onward and onward we went, and still no enemy, much to our surprise. We reached the top of the hill and accomplished what we went there to do, *take possession of that hill at any sacrifice,* as it commanded the town of Corinth (This we *common folk* learned afterwards) ; reaching the top we halted, and were kept at our attention for a long time. I could see our Generals were at fault, but soon now movements commenced. The Battery was brought up, placed in position, a company from each regiment thrown out as skirmishers, the whole line ordered to lie down, and the skirmishers to advance. The Battery was right in the centre of our Battalion,

we supported it. The skirmishers soon passed from our
sight down the hill toward Corinth, in about 5 minutes
crash went a rifle, and then another and another, in a
few minutes it extended along the whole line in front
and the bullets whistled over our heads quite frequently,
two passed through a sapling under which I was lying,
one of them would have been uncomfortably low if I
had been standing up. In a few minutes two wounded
men came limping in, both wounded in the legs, and
later two more, they passed to the rear to the surgeon,
no questions were asked them as we could not leave our
positions. Soon the firing ceased for a while, and then
was resumed farther off. We knew that they were being
driven in, but in a moment Bang Bang went two cannon, and then the explosion of shells. We now waited
anxiously and almost breathlessly, and soon comes in an
orderly with a report that our skirmishers have driven
the enemy in over the next hill when the shells were
thrown among them from an unseen battery some distance in front, and they fell back to their position. And
thus ended the battle so far as we were concerned. But
the Brigade on our left, Johnson's, at the same time
were having a serious fight which we heard all the time
and supposed a general engagement was coming on.
They drove the enemy in, in force. By night, firing had
ceased along the whole line, and we saw no other signs
of battle than two of our wounded being carried by on
stretchers. (And here let me say that the most grue-
some sight I have yet seen is the detail for carrying off
wounded that deliberately marched in front of us all
with yellow badges on their arms). We were then ordered to keep our positions during the night, every man
lying on his arms, with a strong picket guard in front.
During the evening the officers gathered in conversa-

tion, and we almost unanimously came to the conclusion that Corinth was evacuated, or they never would have let us take those positions without a fight as the next day our siege guns could open on Corinth. A feeling of deep disappointment prevailed, as we did not want to go farther South. I felt very badly that night, but laid myself down and tried to sleep, for a long time I could not, but finally did so, and here occurred an incident, that I think tried me well, and as I conducted myself as I would wish to, I will give it. I was aroused from a feverish sleep by firing of guns, hollowing, rattling of wagons, and a most terrible sound generally on our right. I jumped from the ground, ran among the company buckling on my sword meanwhile. I had them in line in a moment. My first thought was where and what is the difficulty, and what shall I do. I saw the confusion was on our right, and no noise in front. I therefore supposed our right flank had been surprised, on this supposition I acted, when the company was fully aroused, I said to them, *Keep cool, don't move an inch, fix bayonets, come to the position of "ready" without cocking the piece, and don't a man fire until I give the order*. All this was done in less time than it takes me to write it, and was all done before the Major reached us which he did by the time the whole battalion was in line. It was pitch dark too, and the noise and firing increased. Just then I heard Capt. Terrell's (of the Battery) loud voice on our right, hollow: Be quiet men! it is only a stampede of the teams! . . . It occurred in the Louisville Legion immediately on our right, and the half asleep soldiers as they jumped into line had fired their pieces at an imaginary enemy in front. It was soon quieted and not much damage done and nobody killed. But the best of the joke was, as we heard afterwards,

the team that caused the stampede ran through our lines
into Corinth and caused a terrible panic there.—All
this was very exciting and did me no good, I slept but
little or none the rest of the night, but laid and listened
to the whistling of locomotives, and playing of bands
in Corinth which I heard very plainly and again re-
assured me that Corinth was evacuated, and they were
only keeping up a strong rear guard to cover their
retreat, and the bands playing at that unusual time was
to make us believe they were still there, but it was a
poor device, as we all knew it was unusual, and caused
us to think and reason.—Well, morning came at last,
and with it a number of deserters, at the same moment
tremendous explosions were heard in Corinth. The deserters said they had completed the evacuation, and
were blowing up their shell &c., our scouts soon came
and confirmed the facts. So ended the "Siege of Corinth". A siege brilliantly planned, and brilliantly executed, notwithstanding its apparent barren effect as it
only drove them away instead of destroying. At first as
I wrote you I was grievously disappointed, but time
and experience have changed my views as well as
others. It is a great pity that they run, but that
could not be prevented. The plan of the siege was to
put ourselves in a strong position before them which
could be held by a small force, and then a large body to
move both to the right and left and come into their
rear and thus destroy their army. The first was accomplished, the latter was prevented by the genius of
Beauregard. He knew he must be destroyed and evacuated. The only other thing we could have done, would
have been to boldly move on their fortifications and
carry them, then pursue them to destruction. This I
believe we could have done, but after seeing their fortifications I am satisfied that it would have cost us from

20 to 30 thousand lives. This Genl Halleck knew, and never intended to attack them in front. 'Tis a pity our plans could not be carried out but still it is much better than a defeat, as we have accomplished what we went to do, take Corinth. As it is the results have been much greater than we at first thought as you have no doubt seen by the papers. So much for Corinth, again to myself. When all this news came, orders came to move into Corinth. By that time I thought I had done my duty, there was to be no more fighting, and I might as well go back, so as soon as we reached their entrenchments and I was assured that all was true, I borrowed a horse, and returned to camp. I found the other Doctor there (we have two) who placed me under treatment, and has cured me.

. . . In a day or two the Battalion was ordered to go in front of Corinth. We went there, and from there to a camp to the east of it. . . . The next day but one we moved and yesterday we reached here about 60 miles, a march that has not had its equal in some respects during the war, and which I intended to describe to you in this letter, but I have orders at this moment to prepare to move so must defer it. We cross the river tomorrow and move *we don't know* where but suppose it to be East Tennessee. . . . Good-bye and believe me as ever

Your loving Husband
Alfred

Camp at Jacksons Ferry
Near Florence, Ala. June 18/62

My Dearest Mary:

I wrote you a long letter day before yesterday which I closed very abruptly under orders to march. But we did not march, and are still here resting, which is about the best thing we can do after our tiresome march here. Troops are crossing the river though now, and I suppose we will get off this aftenoon or tomorrow morning. And as I may not have another opportunity of writing for some time will continue my journal to date. . . .

When I sent the note by Mr. Miller I had a headache, unfortunately next day I was not well and in the evening had a chill. I took quinine next day and the next day we had orders to march, and to prepare for a long one. Here was more trouble for me. Two of our officers left us for home on sick leave, and should I go too? I had a long talk with the Doctor, who told me I had an intermittent fever, that was producing a thorough change in my system, my bowels were getting into good condition, and if I would take strong doses of quinine and brandy the change of air and water would perhaps benefit me, if the exertion of marching would not be too much for me at the start; so I prepared to go. And here let me say that your question about the heat and dust and scarcity of water in our old camp was correct. What little water we could get was unwholesome, and that was the cause of mine and others sickness.

Well we started on the afternoon of the 10th, previously sent our sick that were unable to march to the Hospital at Corinth. We made 10 miles that afternoon through a wilderness, but found good water for the first time for a while. How we enjoyed it, that and the quinine and brandy gave me an appetite. I missed my chill and felt better next morning. We were off early this day, the heat came down terribly, the dust was fully from 3 to 4 inches deep, and you can imagine what an atmosphere we travelled in, 30,000 men stirring it up. I think I can safely say that during our march here I did not breathe a particle of pure air excepting at night.

We still kept through a wilderness and that night reached Iuka [Mississippi]. This is really a beautiful place, a new town with fine chalybite [chalybeate] and sulphur springs; it is a fashionable watering place. But it was almost deserted, I however got here, some fresh milk, and chickens which after our hard fare was delightful. We rested here one day and on the morning of the 13th started again. Now comes the hard part of the march. We soon got out of the continual wilderness I have ever been in since being in the field, and entered the west end of Tuscumbia Valley, a most splendid rolling cultivated country covered with splendid plantations. Here I saw slavery in its real colors for the first time, gangs of from 20 to 50 men and women in their cotton clothes working together in the fields. They would stop and look at us with grinning faces, and I could easily see that they thought us their friends. As we did not halt near any of them I had no conversation with them. It was observable though that we never saw anybody about the residences, they were tightly shut. I did not see more than a dozen white men on the march nor did we pass through any villages. It was one continuous line of large plantations, with palatial residences, nor did we see but very little cotton planted but a great deal of corn and wheat. This country is thoroughly secesh, as I believe the whole South is. I feel disgusted as do all of us at the particular care taken that no one enters any dwellings by the way while we poor fellows are living on hard bread and pork these rascals have their cellars full of wholesome food. We felt an additional disgust since being here at reading in a Cincinnati paper a communication from Gen. Halleck to the Sanitary Commission requesting aid for the suffering women and children about Corinth whose husbands

had been pressed into the rebel service. It is all true they
are suffering, but why not levy on their rich secesh, and
make them support them, even if we can get nothing
from them. Just think of my having to pay 75 cents for
one mess of beets, and $1.00 for two small chickens,
the only thing I could get on the route, and that my
cook had to walk miles to darkey huts for, and since
being here the only vegetables I have had is some
stewed green apples which my man stole from an
orchard. Our Generals manage to get enough but nobody below them can. But to our march. By some mis-
management, which it appears always occurs, our provi-
sion team did not come up and that night our men were
without meat, at least most of them, some had some,
among them myself and my Company had one day
more. But that day had been a hard march, and being
in an open country we had no shade, the mercury about
94, the dust worse and worse, but we found good water
and that saved us. The next morning early we marched
but this day we were in the rear and did not get off till
about 10, in the heat of the day. This was a terrible
day. The dust rose in clouds, so that for a great part of
the time I could not see 10 feet in front of me, we
made frequent and short halts. But the great heat, and
want of meat and want of coffee with some was telling
on the men, and for myself strange to say I got better
and better and stronger as I went. We passed hundreds
of stragglers lying under trees and under fences waiting
for evening to come up. Some were very sick, and here
I saw something of the terrible realities of a hard
march. As we were ascending a steep hill a horseman
rode back and asked for our doctor who rode back
with him. When we reached the top of the hill as I
passed by I saw a poor fellow lying under a tree just

dead! The doctor had not reached him in time. As I
passed I heard the doctor reading from a piece of paper
taken from his pocket, "My name is N. O. Hack, I am
from —— Co., Ohio. If I am killed write to my
mother." What a pang it sent to my heart to think of
that poor mother. We passed many that I don't think
will ever get much farther, in fact I have heard of a
number that died on that day. We halted after marching 8 miles and rested until after 4 P.M., then pushed on
till long after dark and reached the camp at 10 at night.
The absence of the sun and a bright moon revived the
drooping spirits of our men, and would you believe it,
my own company came into camp singing a hymn, a
chorus, it was really beautiful. I lost a number of stragglers that day but they all came up. The entrance to
our camp was the finest military view I ever had. Our
whole Division about 10000 or 12000 men were encamped in one large field, and when we came up they
had their fires all burning. It was the first time, we had
ever been in open ground together so that we could all
see each other. I wanted to see it by daylight, but the
order was, *March at 3½ in the morning*. As soon as
supper was over (we got one day's rations here) the
men were asleep, and Oh how hard it was to arouse
them in the morning. But we were off at the time, and
finished our march to this place by 9 on Sunday morning. Here we are pleasantly fixed and resting preparatory to a long march somewhere, we have turned over
all the men's extra clothing, leaving only what they have
on, a change of under clothes and a blanket, with 3 tents
to a company;—just at this moment we have orders to
pack up and cross the river so must close. Will only say
that I am very well, have lost some flesh but believe I
will gain it on the march. I must say though that I had

a great pleasure this morning. Orders have been issued for all commanders to make a detailed report of the doings of their commands from the Battle of Shiloh to the taking of Corinth. Maj. Carpenter read me his report this morning, and in it he says after speaking in very flattering terms, I give you his words as near as I can recollect: "My 6th Company F commanded by Capt. Hough assisted by Lieut. Stansbury, joined me on the 27th and participated in the arduous duties of the Batt. with a spirit that shows the true soldier, and on the march upon Corinth though both sick and unfit for duty marched or rode in the ambulance, and by their presence and soldierly attention to their duties gave that confidence to their men, that only can be imparted by example, &c., &c." I feel grateful that I have performed my duty. But I must close in a hurry again. You must expect *notes* again now. Kiss the children. Ever your Husband,

Alfred

In Bivouack 7 miles west of Huntsville, Ala.
Sunday, June 29th, 1862
My Dearest Wife:
We arrived here last evening immediately upon which I dropped you a note for fear we should march again early in the morning. But I am happy to say we are to remain here all day and a very pleasant spot we are in. Just in the border of an open wood with cultivated fields in front and rolling hills in the distance, a stream running near, and withal a bright beautiful day with breeze enough to make it pleasant in our shady bivouack. Another element of comfort is abundance of ripe blackberries (the first *ripe* ones we have seen) all around us. I never saw so many in my life. Our whole

army have had their fill and there are enough left within a half mile of us to feed ten times as many. I do not
exaggerate when I say that one man could pick a bushel
in two hours. You cannot imagine how we enjoy them,
the first fruit we have had this season. Our living
though has been better since being on the march. In
spite of orders *against entering houses on any pre-
tence*!! our servants manage to buy chickens and vegetables enough to make us comfortable though to do so
they have to cook at night while we are sleeping, as we
march all day. I am having a glorious dinner prepared
to-day of chicken, beets, new potatoes, onions, stewed
apples, cornbread and butter and blackberries. My
shade is hard at it now.

. . . I have left behind in hospitals between Corinth
and here 16 of my men. I have now absent sick of my
Company 21 men, have 4 sick with me two of whom I
shall leave at Huntsville, the rest like myself have
gained strength, and are in splendid condition although
some of them are very bare of clothes, they have been
allowed to start with only the suit they had on. Some
of them are barefooted and I myself am almost so having my last pair of shoes on and a large hole in one of
them. If we don't get clothes at Huntsville we will be
in a bad plight. I shall not attempt to give as full an
account of our journey from Florence here, as I did of
the one to Florence, but will note the most important
circumstances only, as generally it was much the same as
heretofore. We started from Florence about 9 A.M. and
marched 6 miles, under the hottest sun and heaviest
dust I ever saw. Oh it was terrible, how any of us could
do it I can hardly realize now, hundreds fell out of the
ranks, some never to fall in again, many severe cases of
sunstroke, at the end of 6 miles we reached delightful

cold water in a shady woods, and while resting and enjoying it a thunder storm, with but little rain though,
not enough to lay the dust, passed over us and cooled
the air. Oh how grateful it was. Since then it has not
been so terribly hot, but about as usual. On Thursday
we started on our dusty march, and in the distance we
could see heavy clouds gathering together and hear the
rolling thunder, never did the traveller in the desert
pray more earnestly for rain than did our weary host;
at last it came, the great drops rolling down, our men
bared their heads to receive them, and fairly turned
their faces to the sky that the cooling bath might fall
upon them. But it was refreshing, and then again with
our reinvigoration how we enjoyed the ridiculous in
looking at each other, the dust upon us and almost in
us, turned to yellow mud, which before night dried
upon us. Since then we have had no dust but good hard
roads, a hot sun to be sure but a good breeze. Yesterday
for the first time we marched under a cloudy sky and
you could hardly imagine the difference in the condition
of the men; none appeared to be fatigued at the end of
the march. The sun is the great trouble of our labor. If
I did not keep my head cool with constant bathing from
my canteen I could not bear it. We have had one most
striking and at the same time ridiculous spectacle also;
it was the crossing of Elk river. The river is about 300
yards wide and the water deep enough to reach *considerably* above the knees of a full grown man, and the
bottom covered with sharp stones. We were ordered to
take off our pantaloons, drawers and stockings but to
keep on our shoes. Now just imagine a string of men
a mile long, 4 abreast with their pantaloons off and
shoes on marching along the bank of the river, and
when in the river it was too funny, from bank to bank

this string of men extended, one arm holding the cast-off clothing and musket, the other holding up their coat tails; further remarks are unnecessary. 'Tis well we have something to amuse us. Day before yesterday we encamped about 4 miles west of Athens [Alabama] to which place there is a railroad from Nashville; we fully expected to stop there and write home, and perhaps hear from home, but we were disappointed, we were marched right through, and encamped 4 miles this side, started in the morning and marched 14 miles to this place. I do hope we will stop at Huntsville, but for fear not I write this now to be mailed there. . . . Your loving and faithful

Husband

4

*   *   *   *   *   *   *   *   *   *

WHILE AT HUNTSVILLE, awaiting further moves, Captain Hough was relieved of his command when Captain James B. Mulligan appeared and took charge of his own company once more. Hough was now ordered to Indianapolis to organize a company and bring it into the field, a task which did not prove to be agreeable to him. As he wrote, "For the next nine months I was of very little service to the public, but not through any actions of my own, for with the exception of my having the supreme happiness of being with my family, I was extremely annoyed during the whole time." There were two principal sources of this annoyance: first, he had planned to raise his company and return to the field as rapidly as possible, but learned that he had been put in charge of recruiting for his regiment; secondly, he found himself under the command of Major Samuel K. Dawson of the 19th Infantry. "Of all the impracticables I have ever come in contact with," Hough complained, "Maj. Dawson was pre-eminent. I can only excuse him from being thoroughly demoniac by believing him to have been insane. . . . I was very soon in conflict with him and seeing no prospect of getting my company came very near resigning from the

Regular Army and entering the Volunteer service, in fact would have done so, had not better judgement of my wife prevailed with me."

Before Captain Hough was able to disassociate himself from the Major, whom he regarded as mad, Dawson suspended him from all duty for a period of two weeks without any specified reason. During this period Hough was offered a Colonelcy and command of a new Indiana regiment, upon the recommendation of Governor Morton of that state, but, as Hough later wrote, "before I could receive official notification of my appointment there was such an outcry against me by local aspirants, who objected to a non-resident of Indiana receiving such honors, the Governor yielded to the clamor and my appointment was re-considered. Thus I lost my Colonelcy because I was not a Hoosier."

Hough was now thrown back into the arms of Major Dawson, a situation which he refused to accept. He immediately applied for an assignment in the recruiting service elsewhere and after considerable grumbling, the Major made the assignment which took the Captain to Cleveland, Ohio.

He wrote a single letter from this place, dated November 9, most of which is of a personal nature and not worth reproducing, except for some of his comments on his failure at recruiting. "I am satisfied from what I see here and what I hear from other recruiting officers both regular and volunteer, that no more recruiting can be done. What may be done by transferring from the volunteers to us I cannot say, but that is the *only* way we can fill, and that I think the Government will insist upon, but that will take some time to do. There is great opposition on the part of State authorities and volunteer officers to our getting their men, and it is a very unpleasant duty on our part to try, but the men are willing if they will permit them. I had started to work in the camp here, with fair prospects of success, when I was met by an order from Gov. Tod to prevent regular officers from enlisting in the camps until further orders from him. He has no doubt written to Washington to have the order suspended and I expect he will succeed. So it goes, everything is in the dark for the regular army."

During the same month, Captain Hough was assigned to duty at Fort Wayne, Indiana, while he continued to wait for the organization of his own company. During his stay there he was sent to Detroit to help quell a race riot which had proved to be too serious for local authorities. This was accomplished with two first lieutenants, Morris and Hays, and seventy-five men. Order was restored in a single day and the men returned to Fort Wayne. Shortly thereafter Captain Hough's company was organized and on March 15, 1863, he sent his family back to Philadelphia and took his newly formed group to Murfreesboro, Tennessee, for action in the field. Upon his arrival he wrote his first letter home from his new post, describing his trip to Tennessee and his recently acquired company.

> In Camp near Murfreesboro, Tenn.
> Monday night March 23/63

My Dearest Wife

I am in my tent, my little camp stove burning brightly or rather warmly, and a heavy rain falling outside. I am very well, and my company is well, my trip was a very quick and successful one, having but one mishap, losing one of my boxes containing some camp equipage, but not seriously inconveniencing me. Mr. [1st Lieut. Lewis T.] Morris and Mr. [1st Lieut. John B.] Hays are well, and we mess together. . . . My quick trip has been of advantage to my reputation as a soldier. The morning you left me at Cleveland, two Companies of the 16th Infty passed through there, and they have not yet arrived, four companies of the 18th left Cincinnati four days before I left Detroit and they are not here either. The Commanding officer of the 16th called on me to-day to get a report of my journey for the purpose of making a report of the delay of his detachment to Headquarters, complaining of the delay and comparing their work with mine. So "Rosy" [1] will know I am here anyhow. As to the prospects for the future I can not tell anything except that there don't appear to be any prospect of a forward movement from here. Rosecrans has drawn in his lines, and the whole army is encamped in a close line of battle, splendid fortifications are immediately in the rear of us and an immense supply of stores are here and more coming, therefore I don't think there is any prospect of our moving backward either. I think Rosecrans argues that they must attack us, or fall back as the country is exhausted of supplies, and if they do attack he is ready for them, this is a splendid army much improved since I left it. The enemy may move in our rear and cut off the supplies, but we have enough, and he will let them go, and trust to the army in Kentucky to take care of them, if they do pass us. This is the reasoning here, and an attack on us at any moment will not surprise us. As I write I hear picket firing in the front, and we may have a fight before

[1] Major General William S. Rosecrans, commanding the Fourteenth Army Corps, Army of the Cumberland.

morning, but all is conjecture, so you must take this for my summary of war news. Now for my journey. We left Detroit on Monday night reached Indianapolis on Tuesday afternoon and laid over there till 9 at night. . . . I reached Louisville on Wednesday morning and staid till Friday morning, to get my men paid, which was done and they have come into the field with light hearts in consequence, many of them sending money home, they behaved well none of them getting on a spree. In fact I have a good company and am much pleased with them. . . . I left Louisville on Friday morning the day after the capture of the train by Greenvilles.[2] I was hoping they would attack again. I was ready for them, but we arrived safely at Nashville by dark and after getting quarters for my men, and supper, I got transportation by rail to Murfreesboro, through much labor, and got to bed at a miserable hotel, weary and tired by 12. Was off next morning at 5 on top of freight cars reached Murfreesboro at 11 and marched out to camp about 1½ miles, got into camp nicely before night; have been hard at work ever since fixing up, and now feel almost as if I had not been away everything seems so natural around me. My men work well and my company is much complimented. . . . Capt. [Lewis] Wilson is in command of the Battallion. He is a good officer but I miss Maj. Carpenter.[3] I am next in rank at present, and if any thing should happen to him [Wilson] and not to me, I should be in command, which I would not wish to be for a while yet. Now my dearest I must close. . . .

Alfred

[2] Alluding to the same incident in his autobiography, Hough calls them bushwhackers.

[3] Killed in action at battle of Murfreesboro, Tennessee, December 31, 1862. (Official Army Register for 1863, p. 97)

Murfreesboro, Tenn. March 30/63

My Dearest Mary:

. . . I have nothing new to tell you. I am living the usual camp life, eat, sleep, drill, and study, no signs of any fighting as yet. I feel almost as if I had not been away from the Battallion everything seems so natural excepting the absence of Maj Carpenter, and that I feel much. My new position of acting field officer is also new to me. Capt. Wilson is again on duty, but I am second in command and under the order here, acting as colonel, which still gives me a horse, I don't know how long it will last, but I hope some time yet as it is very comfortable to ride on drill, instead of marching at double quick for an hour or two. Oh you ought to see Morris after drill, Hays remarks to him are funny in the extreme. Morris is a fine officer, I was very fortunate in getting him. He and Hays afford me a great deal of amusement. They occupy the tent next to me, and the contrast between theirs and mine is marked, mine is fixed up with a great deal of comfort about it, to accomplish which took a deal of work, they just turned in and "staid" with nothing but their cots and trunks, the first night they stuck their candle in the ground, the next they had got a chip to fasten it on, and the only other furniture they have as yet is a wash basin, and an empty box for a seat, and to hear them abuse one another for not getting things is too amusing. We are having an influx of officers just now, as fast as they arrived they were temporarily assigned to camp and for duty, but now all the places are filled, and several are here waiting orders and more coming. Capt. [Gideon C.] Moody and [Thomas] Cummings are both here, the latter is on duty but Capt. Moody is waiting orders, I cannot imagine why they were sent here, but I suppose they will be sent to headquarters on staff duty which is merely clerking. I am glad I am not on the list. So many green officers coming gives us older ones a deal of work. A school of instruction has been ordered, and I am detailed as one of the instructors, recitations in the evenings they commence tomorrow, so there is more work for me. . . .

Alfred

Camp near Murfreesboro, Tenn.
April 12 1863

My Dearest Wife:

I have yours of April 5th this morning, it made quite a quick trip, and most welcome it is. You say my last was dated March 23rd. I don't see how it is that letters from here are so irregular, it is the complaint of the whole army that letters *from* the army are very slow and frequently miscarry, while letters to the army rarely fail. My last to you, a short one I fear was captured by the Rebs, as they "guerrillaed" a train from here to Nashville last week. I am very well but have been very busy for the last week, was in command, but Capt. [Augustus H.] Plummer arrived yesterday and released me. I am now second in command and still have a horse. Both Capt. Moody and Capt. [Reuben D.] Mussey have been detached on mustering service, at Division Headquarters, and if Capt. [Edward L.] Smith from the Army of the Potomac don't come with his Company (which it is said is on the way) I shall remain second in command, which will be very comfortable. But still I am not as happy here as I was under the old regime. We have a fine Battallion of men, though a small one, but all of the old officers leaving and new and inexperienced ones being in their places makes work and anxiety for the few of us that do know our business. Capt. Plummer I like and think he will suit. The other officers are making and in time I think all will be right. You ask why we are not with [Major General Gordon] Granger who is at Franklin, [Tennessee] that is another Granger, one Granger was in command while Rosecrans was absent, but now Rosecrans has returned as I told you before, we did not like our Granger and are in trouble to-day hearing that he is to take command of our Brigade, relieving Col. Sheppard who we all like. I regret it very much as Col. Sheppard had taken especial notice of me, and I am told was instrumental in getting the ranking officers over me detached for the purpose of giving me rank with the Battallion. The officers were of course willing to go, but the Col. helped them. Col. S. was very kind to me and I don't know Granger and don't like his looks. . . . I have no war news to tell you, nothing occurring here, all is quiet, and we are living as if we were in camp in Pennsylvania, barring not quite so good eating, provisions, I mean home food, is getting scarce. We have our dress parades and guard mountings in style, and all is as merry as if thousands of our friends did not lie buried almost beneath our feet, in fact some of them do, such is war. Men can get habituated to anything. I hear Granger had a fight at Franklin, whipping the rebs. Maybe they will attack us, if they don't I see no prospect of a fight here soon, and I don't think we can move forward, at least until Burnsides makes some demonstrations on our left. . . .

Your loving husband,

Alfred

Murfreesboro, Tenn.
April 16th 1863

My Dearest Wife:

. . . We are still in the same old camp, living the
same life we have been, making ourselves as comfortable and happy as we can, I being second in command
have a very comfortable position. Mr. Morris has the
command of the Company. Capt. Plummer don't do
much out of the office, and I drill the Battallion generally, he has only taken command once; and then
(privately he told me) he did not know anything about
it as he had never drilled a battallion since he left West
Point, and is studying tactics like a school boy. He is
very much of a gentleman, and we have a feeling in
common as he grieves after his wife and talks about
her. He has no mess yet and is stopping with us. Morris
and Hays make my mess very lively; I have my own
tent, and live a quiet dignified life, the younger officers
rarely visit me unless invited, but Morris and Hays
next door have a crowd around them all the time, and
when we have our meals under an awning back of my
tent, their conversation often makes good any deficiency
in the quality of victuals. Morris can already "take off"
all the characters in the Brigade. To-day [1st Lieut.
Alfred] Curtis got a box from home at Indianapolis
and generously sent us all a piece of cake from the
same. Morris immediately exclaimed that if Curtis
could get a box he did not see why he could not, transportation or no transportation, and he should immediately write home that he was starving on pork and hard
bread, or as the soldiers call it "sheet iron and sow
belly", and he knew his mother could not rest till he
had a supply of "cans". I hope his strategy will be suc-

cessful. I have experienced but one phase of new life
since my last, and as that was interesting to me I will
try to give you an account of it. Last Monday I as acting Lieut Col. took my turn as officer in charge of
pickets, which means that (though) I had the care and
charge of the picket lines in front of our corps. It was
most laborious duty but interesting. Our front extends
about a mile and a half and there are two lines, the
Infantry line about a two miles in front of our camps,
and a Cavalry line about two miles in front of them. To
visit them makes a ride of at least ten miles, and this I
had to do four times in the 24 hours, once on taking
charge with the old officers, once just before night,
once in the night, and again the next morning on turning the charge over to the new officer. The duty is to
inspect, give orders, correct any deficiencies and make a
report of the state of affairs as found. My night tour
was rough in the extreme, it rained hard, and was very
dark, to be riding alone in the dark, and be challenged
every once in a while by a voice coming from a man I
could not see and hear the click of his musket, was exciting in the extreme, but I got through all safely. I
started from camp at 2 o'clock in the morning and got
back at daylight; during my afternoon inspection I had
a conversation with a darkey which will give you a
pretty good idea of affairs, where an army has been any
time; you must know that the whole region about here
is desolated, houses are shattered or destroyed, fences
all gone, beautiful gardens that were, thrown out in the
vast field for army teams to run over, nothing planted,
and only the grass looking green. Well about half way
between our Infantry and Cavalry pickets there are
the negro huts of a plantation, the planter's house is

some distance off and deserted. I noticed as I passed, the negro women about the huts, and some cows penned up among them as you would see in a town, and almost as far as your eyes could reach one vast field without fences of what was once a splendid farm; near the wood was a negro man collecting some few rails that were left, and building a fence around one of the fields, and in the field a woman ploughing, as it was the first sign of work I had seen anywhere out of army work I stopped and the following conversation ensued:

Myself: Well uncle, are you going to raise some corn?

Darkey: Yes sah, Ise a-gwine to see if I can't raise something to eat for us.

Myself: Who does this plantation belong to?

Darkey: Mr. Kearny.

Myself: Where does he live?

Darkey: In Murfreesboro.

Myself: Is he Union or secesh?

Darkey: Well massa, dey is all about the same, when one is Union, dey is all Union, and when one is secesh, dey is all secesh.

Myself: Did he order you to do this work?

Darkey: Lord bress you massa he aint done nothin for us since you comed here, and we had to look out for ourselves.

Myself: Well how have you got along?

Darkey: Oh pretty well considerin, General [D. S.] Stanley, let us have some corn dat he had over from his feedin his horses, and let us keep a few cows, and den dere was right smart of hogs here, and he gibe us some salt to put dem down wid, and if you don't only hab a fight here till I can raise some corn, we hab enough to get along with till den.

I have run out my sheet and will stop. . . .

Your loving husband,

Alfred

Headquarters 2d Div. 14th A. C.
Murfreesboro, May 28, 1863

My Dearest Mary: [4]

. . . I am really very happy here, my duties interest me much, and I have the satisfaction of knowing that I am useful to the Government. And then the very effort to send me back has given me a good character on the record. The application to send me back has been returned to Capt. Plummer, who shewed it to me, and I have taken a copy of it. It is too long to send you a full copy, but I will give you the pith of it. Capt. Plummer

[4] Toward the end of April Captain Hough was able to obtain a brief leave and hastened home to Philadelphia for a few days with his family. He returned to duty again about the middle of May but was not happy with his old assignment, for, as he said, "the Battallion was not like it was of old, Maj. Carpenter was dead, and the best of its officers were detailed on staff duty." Hough now decided to apply for staff duty, even though he might have to serve at a lower rank. "I informed a friend at Head Quarters that I would accept a position and was at once appointed a Commissary of Musters at Head Quarters of Second Division Fourteenth Corps, Maj. Genl. [James S.] Negley commanding, to relieve an officer found to be incompetent. The duties of this position were to decide upon and fix legally the status in the U. S. Service of officers and men raised by the State Authorities." There was some difficulty in the transfer. The field officers objected strenuously at the prospect of losing subordinates to the staff. Looking back on the action, Hough admitted that "My leaving the Battallion was not without opposition, for after I had received the order to go, and had obeyed it and had reported for duty, Capt. Plummer, Comdg. the Battallion made application to have me returned to it. This effort failed, but as it was the means of giving me a good official record, I will give a history of it, that my children may know I did my duty well with my Company while in command of it. . . ." Hough's letter of May 28, 1863, furnishes the details of his change of duty.

says: "Almost any other officer of the Batt. could be better spared than Capt. Hough. He is an excellent line officer and is well fitted to command a company or a regiment". Genl King endorses it and says: "The services of Capt. A. L. Hough 19th U. S. Infty are necessary with his Company. If the best officers of my command are to be selected for staff duties, who are to take charge of my men in action". Genl Rousseau adds "I heartily approve the objections and suggestions urged by Genl. King". Genl. Thomas on top of all this says simply "Application *not* recommended". Genl Rosecrans finished it with "Respectfully returned not recommended, Capt. Hough's services are indispensable in his present position". What a record they have made for me. I value that paper highly. It has made quite a talk here, and withal there has been no hard feeling and we are all good friends. I am more than ever glad that I have got away now. [1st Lieut. Thomas] Cummings has received his commission as Captain! Just think of it. The few good officers that are left feel their position deeply and would resign most of them if they could, and all trying to get on other duty. I think my position here now is secure, and, will be permanent. I would have preferred getting nearer you but that could not be. What our next move will be I cannot say. It all depends upon Grant's success or failure, we are waiting anxiously for him. I fear he will be overpowered, it would be dreadful if he were. Hooker appears to have been beaten badly [at Chancellorsville]. Who will lead them next? The army of the Potomac appears to be the grave of would be great men; but I hope it will yet redeem itself.

[Clement L.] Vallandingham [*sic*] passed through here but I did not see him, he was hurried through, if he had been turned loose here he could not have lived, the soldiers would have killed him, as it was, at Nashville the 93rd Ohio had to be kept under guard to prevent them from mobbing him. My present position brings me in constant communication with officers of volunteers I can speak freely of the strong sentiments entertained by them. They detest Copperheadism, and the heartiest ones I find are from Ohio the home of Vallandingham. The General treats me very kindly, asked me to ride with him last evening which I did, and had a pleasant time. I have worked all day every day since I have been here; shall be kept constantly at work for about three weeks yet, after that my berth will be comparatively easy. . .

As ever yours lovingly,

Alfred

Sunday evening June 21st 1863

My Dearest Mary

I have to-day repudiated Pennsylvania and announced myself as a Jerseyman, notwithstanding Miss Anna E. Dickinson called it that "mean little State". Just to think that the Governor of the great State of Pennsylvania should be compelled to ask that the 3 regiments of hers in the army [5] might be sent back home for the protection of her borders because her own people would not arouse from their money making to do it themselves. Of course he wont get them, but think of his being compelled to ask it. The Pennsylvanians here just wish that the rebels would make a raid right through the State and rip it from North to South, and then we would see whether our people were fit to be battled for. Oh what a disgrace that they should sniffle

[5] In consequence of Lee's invasion of Pennsylvania.

about volunteering for six months or six days when their very soil was invaded. But language cannot express my indignation,—later news tells us the rebels have not advanced far 'tis a great pity, for I am convinced that nothing but suffering the reality of war will ever wake up the Rip Van Winkles. Having fallen back upon my native state, I mounted my horse and proceeded to find some Pennsylvanians to abuse. I went to see Jesse first, and found him and his Keystone companions of whom there are several, quite as indignant as myself. I abused *their* state till I got in quite a good humor. Well I hope all will go right with you, that some good will come out of the desperation of the rebels, that the people will rally in such strength that Lee will be overwhelmed. We feel here as though we were only guarding a "side gate", Grant and Banks on the Mississippi, and Hooker on the Potomac, have either to move on or fall back, they *must* accomplish something tangible, or the reverse, while we are only watching the side entrance to prevent a fire in the rear. If Hooker and Grant succeed we shall have but little to do, but if they fail, oh what a blow will be struck at us. Our devoted band will either achieve wonders, or be destroyed, such is our belief here, and with such belief we watch the course of events with anxiety. Nothing out of the usual course has occurred since my last, excepting a military execution in our division. I witnessed it, and was surprised at the solemnity, and decorum of the scene, it was really very impressive to see the prisoner with his chaplain, walking along the line of 6000 soldiers at parade [rest] followed by the firing party, who were to launch him into eternity, and his coffin carried by 4 men, the whole preceded by a band playing the dead march, and at the very head the Provost Marshal on horseback. I must say that such a scene must have an effect on soldiers. The poor fellow was penitent, and died bravely, he deserted and joined the enemy and was afterwards captured.

My own personal position continues comfortable. Also my health, to let you know how well I am you must only know that every day last week after doing my office work, I was on drill for 4 or 5 hours in the afternoon, riding hard all the time and the sun pouring down terribly. Yet I would come to camp and eat a hearty supper and sleep as soundly as ever I did, (I was just going to say "alongside of you", but that gives me such a fit of homesickness that I wont say it). Just think of my sleeping under two blankets every night, but such is the case; this is a wonderful country. You want to know what a "Commissary of Musters" is. I will tell you. All volunteers, after being raised in their respective states, have to be "mustered" into the U. S. Service by a U. S. officer. This has been done so irregularly during the war, that, a department of Musters has been established, and every Division in the army has an assistant Commissary of Musters, whose duties are to muster all volunteers as they enter the service or are promoted, and to give all information on the subject of mustering for pay, &c., &c. The duties are responsible and at times laborious. Now these are strictly my only duties, if I choose to stand on my *right,* but all staff officers are expected to act as aide to their General if he wishes it, and as Gen. Negley does I give him all the assistance in my power and he avails himself of it. On drill he works me pretty hard, so much so that he has directed me to have another horse issued to me, so that I shall have two for use. I have given you as lucid an explanation as possible. . . .

As ever yours,
Alfred

Murfreesboro Wednesday morning
June 24th 1863

My Own Dear Wife: [6]

We received marching orders last night, and within an hour from this time this whole army leaving only a

[6] On June 23 Negley's command received its marching orders and Hough terminated what he regarded as a pleasant stay at Murfreesboro. The campaign started off auspiciously enough for the Captain who now had not only a colored servant, but two horses for his own use. In his Autobiography he describes this latest movement of his division. "Before receiving marching order I attached myself a 'contraband' by name John Thomas. John was a runaway slave who like thousands of others fled to the army, he remained with me throughout the war, and was ever faithful and true, he was my groom, my cook, my washerman, my body servant, in fact, my all, through every vicissitude. Fully equipped for the campaign with two horses, a limited amount of baggage, a clerk and John Thomas, I reported ready for the march as the Division went into column, on the 24th day of June 1863. . . . Our Division with the 1st Division in advance took the road toward Manchester through Hoover's Gap, the remainder of the army took other roads southward and we had a quiet march for two days, without incident of note.

"At Hoover's Gap, a depression in the line of hills stretching across the country, our advance was resisted by some artillery with infantry support. We brushed this away after a sharp fight, the 1st Division and principally the Regular Brigade did the work, our Division was in reserve. I was sent to the front to receive orders if necessary and was present at the fight, the Regular Brigade charged gallantly, and drove the enemy, suffering considerably, three men of my Company were wounded and two killed. During this affair my horse fell with me, and striking my knee on a rock it left a bruise on the bone below the knee, that I did not suffer much from at the time, but which subsequently gave me much trouble and occasionally does yet. Before night we had cleared the wood and both Divisions passed the Gap and went into Camp on the other side. Without further difficulty except the rain and mud we reached Manchester, [Tennessee,] and after a short stay, again took the road with our Division at the head.

"Our Brigade with a battery of six pieces attached was sent forward garrison in the Fort will be heading southward. The mails may be interrupted, and you may not hear from me again for some time. We may have some terrible battles to fight, and we may find no enemy near. Our destination I know not. But you will no doubt have the news by the papers before this reaches you. Write to me as usual and the letters will follow us up. I will keep you advised of my movements. . . .

Alfred

Elk River Ford
6 miles below Tullahoma
July 2nd noon

My Dearest Mary

I write this on the battle field.[7] We have been pursuing the enemy for the last three days over bad roads, and fighting all the time, they have checked us here, by

---

as an advanced guard. I was ordered with it, with directions to push it forward rapidly, and clear the way of any of the enemys rear guard we should find. The first day we met with no resistance, a few men only were seen who fled before our skirmishers. . . .

"During the next three days we had lively times. Our road ran through rolling country well wooded with an occasional clearing, the enemy had left a horse battery with mounted support to annoy our march, and right well they did it. Having to march with a deployed line in front extending into the woods on both sides, our progress was necessarily slow, and from behind every elevation we would receive messages from the Battery, it would always leave upon our approach and take a new position. We still could always find it again. How I longed for more cavalry to send after it. . . .

"On the 2nd of July at the crossing of Elk River six miles from Tullahoma we met with more resistance, and the whole Division went into action."

[7] Rosecrans had moved against Bragg on June 24 but had failed to engage him in general battle. The Confederates temporarily halted the Federal force at Elk River by burning the bridge at that point. Rosecrans asserted that in the whole action "our losses in killed and wounded will not exceed 500. The loss of the enemy may be safely put at 1,000 killed and wounded and 1,000 prisoners, 7 pieces of artillery, 500 or 600 tents." Rosecrans to Stanton, July 4, 1863, *O.R.*, Series I, Vol. XXIII, Part I, p. 403.

burning the bridge, and the river is too high to ford, we have had quite a fight here this morning, our loss has been very small so far, but our men are much fatigued, the weather is very hot, this is only one column of the army, other columns are on other roads, we did not come through Tullahoma, but passed it to the left, another column is there, they are in full retreat, but fighting hard. We are resting, and I do not know whether we shall attempt to cross on pontoons or whether we will wait a day for the river to fall. The party around me is unique in the extreme, Gen. Negley and staff with attendants lying on the grass, near us a group of rebel prisoners, our horses tied near us, a short distance off the wounded being taken care of &c., &c. I have worked hard, very hard, and am still well; shot and shell have passed near me but as yet I have passed unscathed. I write this in hopes of sending it by a courier, have not seen our baggage for four days, found this paper in the house near me, or would not have written, as I don't know when I can send. I can write no more as the General wants me. Good bye and God bless us all is the prayer of

Your affectionate husband,

Alfred [8]

[8] It was during the fighting at Elk River that Hough had his first words with General George H. Thomas, whose senior aide he would be after the war, and with whom he would serve until that famous man died in 1870. Hough relates, in his Autobiography, how the enemy had been pushed across the river and was being shelled by Negley's artillery. At this juncture General Thomas came up and commenced questioning Hough, who had just been detailed to carry a message to him. "This was my first conversation with him, he asked me if I had been with the advance, and if so all about the movement. I told him all. He listened attentively, asking me leading questions, and ended by directing me to tell Genl. Negley to cease firing as it was no use wasting ammunition across the river. I left him and did so. We lost a good many men in this fight, including some prisoners taken at the first onset, before we knew their strength or position. The next day the

HEAD-QUARTERS, SECOND DIVISION
Fourteenth Army Corps.
July 5th 1863

My Dearest Wife:

Just at this time one year ago I started, northward, homeward bound. With what ecstatic feelings I turned from my comrades, filled with the hope of seeing you and ours. Now how different, southward bound, making the distance between us more and more every day. "But all is well that ends well" and when we meet again, may we not be separated for so long a time. We are in camp to-day at the foot of the Cumberland Mountains, S. E. from Tullahoma. We intended to reach the top of the Mountains yesterday but after toiling all the afternoon, it was found to be impossible, the mud, rocks and fallen timber could not be overcome, so we countermarched and got into camp at the foot of the Mountain just after dark. Our pioneers are clearing the road to-day and to-morrow I suppose we shall start again. It was a fearfully hard day's work, and oh how good it is to rest to-day this Sabbath, but it still rains, coming down in torrents as I write. The

---

water fell and we pushed across the river, our Division still in the advance, but saw no enemy. On the 4th of July we reached the Cumberland Mountains, and began to ascend, but finding the woods completely obstructed by fallen trees and rocks our progress was very slow. While at work clearing away the obstructions Genl. Negley received orders to return to the place below and go into Camp."

As a matter of fact, Negley himself made the decision to return. In a report written on July 8, the general explained that "from the lateness of the hour and almost impassable condition of the road, I deemed it impracticable to reach water that night by going farther. I therefore ordered the troops to descend, and encamped at the foot of the mountain. Here I was directed to remain until further orders." (Major General James S. Negley's Report of July 8, 1863, *O.R.*, Series I, Vol. XXIII, Part I, p. 442.) It was from this camp, at the foot of the Cumberland mountains, that Hough wrote his next letter home.

rains have been the means of preventing us from entirely intercepting Hardee's [9] Corps, which I can see now was part of our campaign. We have driven them hard all the time, but they having the start, destroyed the bridges, and the swollen streams could not be forded, we would have to wait for them to subside, and then another rain before we reached the next stream, we aimed to get into the mountains before they did, but they passed over on the 3rd of July, and will be safe in Chattanooga before we get over. If we could have had fine weather I verily believe we would have destroyed Hardee's Corps this side of the mountains. This has been the hardest work I ever experienced, and Gen. Negley says the hardest one he ever had at this season of the year. We left Murfreesboro on the 24th ult I believe and it has rained every day but two since we left. The elements obstructed us, but we pushed the enemy so hard they could do nothing to stop us except burning the bridges, until they got into the Mountains, and there they have felled trees across the passes, that will take us some time to clear away. We are still in the advance on this road, and what we will have to do when we get across I do not know, but suppose the different corps will join, and make a combined attack on Bridgeport or Chattanooga; the fall of either will carry both of these strongholds; we have been eminently successful in driving them across the Mountains, compelling them to evacuate two strongly fortified towns Shelbyville & Tullahoma (good depots for us) and opening up a large space of country in a few days with but little loss to ourselves, but at the same time we feel disappointed at not having destroyed Hardee's Corps, which was in

[9] Lieutenant General William J. Hardee, C. S. A., who had resigned his United States Army commission January 31, 1861.

the rear. But the more we get the more we want, when
we started, there was not a man or officer that I know
of, but what expected we should have had two or three
heavy battles with great loss on our side before getting
this far, and most certainly if we had not surprised
them, this would have been the case, they were not prepared for our ordnance from the direction we came on
them. We are in great anxiety to-day about the battle
of Gettysburg; we have a despatch that they are fighting, "with success on our side so far" but this is so
indefinite that we are almost sick with anxiety to hear
more. The result there and at Vicksburg will have a
great effect upon our army. Almost all of the prisoners
we have taken are very desponding [*sic*] and appear
glad to be taken especially Tennesians [*sic*], who all
say they do not want to leave the state, and many of
the Tenn. troops would not do so if they were not
driven by cavalry. One thing is certain you need not
fear of another retreat on our part like Buell's of last
year. No army could live in Tennessee this year, we
bring our supplies after us, but what little there is in
the country we are taking, but there aint much left, the
people complain as much of the rebel army as they do
of ours. My position on the staff is much more interesting than my former one as it affords me greater oppor-
tunities of seeing and hearing what is going on. I shall
have much to tell about when we meet again. The General keeps me busy, and I have been in the saddle constantly, many scenes are laughable, but some are almost
heartrending. An incident yesterday morning I must
relate, as it shows the temper of the rebel women, their
impudence and arrogance as also, the nonplussing of
your humble servant. We camped last night at the house
of a man named Pennington, an officer in the rebel

army, his wife a regular southern Alabama woman remaining at home to run the plantation. There had been some cavalry there before we got there and pretty nearly cleaned the plantation, having had a skirmish with the enemy near by, and whipped them. There were a few sheep left which our comissary [sic] seized. Well when we arrived Mrs. P. asked Gen. Negley for some bacon and bread, as hers had "all been stolen"; he gave it to her, which she received saucily. I however got into conversation with her, and palavering awhile got her into a good humor and had quite a pleasant conversation; the next morning early as we were eating breakfast on the lawn under her window, (some of the mutton on the table) she put her head out of the window, and called me. I was smacking my lips from the effects of the juicy mutton, and approached her; she said to me, "Captain I merely wished to remind you that you have not sent me any of *my sheep* for breakfast!" I was taken back for a moment but replied, I beg your pardon, madam, for not reminding the comissary [sic] of it, but will still do so if you wish it; she said it made no difference, and retired with a vindictive smile. I must confess I was "taken aback". You must not think that pillaging is encouraged, not at all, the officers in the name of the Government seize the property, and it is distributed regularly, but pillaging is prevented as strictly as possible, and the guilty ones punished. Our army is living well, having regular rations with us and fresh ones provided from the country. . . . I don't say anything about our fighting but we have had plenty of it. I have been in the front during all of our advance, and have done my duty, that is all I have to say. Am looking anxiously for a letter from you. . . .

                                                            Alfred

Dechard Tenn.[10]
July 9th 1863

My Own Dearest Mary

. . . My letters, if you got them, will have given you an account of our doings up to Monday last when we were in camp at the foot of the mountains having in vain tried to ascend them, it is very fortunate now that we did not get over the mountains, as we should have suffered for food. We have entirely outstripped our transportation, and the increasing rains prevented our supplies reaching us. In consequence of this the pursuit is abandoned for the present, and we are resting, waiting for supplies to come up and the railroad to be repaired to this point so that a depot of supplies can be

[10] On July 8th Negley's division went into camp at Dechard, Tennessee. "The first object of the campaign had failed," Hough later wrote, "the enemys line was across our line of march with Tullahoma fortified for a centre. We had evidently intended to turn their right flank and intercept their retreat to Chattanooga, but the rains had so impeded our march that they got away without serious damage leaving little but an empty camp."

The encampment at Dechard was welcome, however, for the troops were badly in need of food and they now had an opportunity to forage for it. The policy of seizing food wherever it could be found was now adopted and for this Hough was happy. As he wrote, "I was glad to find a change of policy had taken place since my former campaigns, we levied on the country for supplies, and did not suffer for food, our Commissaries and Quartermasters regularly seized such supplies as were needed and could be had. Without this action we should have suffered or been compelled to stop, as when we reached Dechard we had been out of supplies for ten days, our supply train having been unable to get through the muddy roads. . . .

"At Dechard our Division was very comfortably arranged, the troops close together on one side of the railroad and the Head Quarters on the other side, some of the Officers had houses and others plenty of tent room. Genl. Thomas's Head Quarters were at a plantation about a half a mile from us, other troops were in the neighborhood and the whole army was within reach. The country around showed signs of the desolation of war, but at best it was not attractive. The curse of slavery showed itself, there was very little attempt at improvement, though nature had done much toward making it pleasant."

established here or at Tullahoma. Our men have now been for ten days without food, excepting what few hogs and cows can be found in this country we are seizing everything we can find, and what the people are to do for food I cannot imagine. We moved our camp to this point yesterday 6 miles for better location and good water besides we are on the railroad, and as soon as it is repaired to this point, we will get the first supplies. We are in the midst of rejoicing at the good news from the east and Vicksburg. We have done a good work too but not what should have [been] done, if the rains had not fallen. We have done all in the power of troops to do. We have driven and demoralized them but oh! if we only could have caught them! Bragg having escaped us for the present and being safe in Chattanooga or gone east, I suppose we shall stop here till we get entirely supplied, and then make another dash and through. The successes elsewhere may though cause a change in our movements but we cannot tell. Our army is still in fine condition notwithstanding our want of supplies. Such cheers as went up from these hungry stomachs at the good news you should have heard; we expect supplies tonight, and then they will get their fill. Blackberries appear to be the principal food to-day. I personally am living pretty well, having brought a good supply but my living is expensive, I could not get into a mess to suit me, so am living by myself have to keep two servants, one for the horses (I have two) and one to cook. I am in a house for the first time we are occupying Bragg's old quarters here, (there are only 12 houses in the place). I opened my office again and have had quite a rush of business, some few nine months men we have to muster out. I hope to get all my writing up while here so as to have a clean sheet for field work again when we get started. I like staff duty in the field immensely, to carry important orders to Colonels and Generals, and "see that they are properly executed" suits me, but they carry me very near the balls and shells sometimes, which are not *very* interesting, at least not enough so as to cause me to be anxious to be near them. I had a letter from John also to-day same date as yours he speaks of the apathy in Pennsylvania, but I am so disgusted with it that I can't bear to talk about it. I should think the people of Pennsylvania would hardly dare to hold up their heads when they met—New Yorkers. But the enemy have been beaten without them thank God for his mercies. I am a little sorry though they did not get Harrisburg before they retreated. I had no fear but what they would have to retreat, and the farther they got north the worse it would be for them. I suppose you are in the midst of excitement, joy at the defeat of Lee and grief at the losses of friends of which there must be many—but enough of war. . . . faithfully and lovingly,

Alfred

Dechard Tenn
July 12th 1863

My Own Dearest Mary:

. . . As I told you all about ourselves in my last letter I can only add we are still at Dechard, that is, our Division. The rest of the army are in different camps within a radius of 20 miles, all resting and waiting for supplies which are now coming up. Reconnoitering parties have gone forward and will report in a day or two. We *believe* Bragg has gone to Richmond, and if so I think it possible our destination may be changed, right straight over the Mountains into East Tennessee.

At any rate I am satisfied whatever the result may be east, that either we will go south or east as soon as we are again ready for the march. I most sincerely trust the latter. Grant has triumphed most gloriously [at Vicksburg] has he not? What a proud time it must have been for him after so many months of anxiety. You appear to have been successful East to a certain extent but a decisive battle is yet to be fought. God grant it may be successful. We have made wonderful strides in the last three weeks, if we can only keep it up now, we will soon tumble the would-be Confederacy, but if we lull and allow them to recover from their shock, another army will have to be raised, to renew the struggle. How proud I feel of you when reading your letter. Your opinions of the men of Philadelphia, in fact of Pennsylvania were honestly expressed, and when danger appeared really to be upon you, to hear you speak out so boldly and honestly makes my heart leap with joy. . . . I think Philadelphia will not be reached. It would not do for me to be home now, I know I should quarrel with many of my friends. I never in my life have felt such mortification and indignation as I have felt since hearing of the conduct of the men of Pennsylvania, I have no hesitation in saying, and will say it openly to *every* able bodied man of military age who did not offer themselves that they do not deserve to be free. It would be but justice if they could be punished, without their patriotic brothers suffering also, for them to be crushed entirely by the invaders of their soil, they should be made to know and feel what war is, and what the patriots of the country suffer, as much for their benefit as their own. . . . Good-bye dearest, God bless you and yours is the prayer of yours lovingly,

                                                    Alfred

Dechard Tenn
July 14th 1863

My Dearest Mary:

I have your letter of the 3rd which breathes a more
hopeful tone than your previous one. A great weight
must be lifted off your shoulders in Pennsylvania. The
invaders have been driven off from your sleep burthened
soil. How much has been accomplished within the last
two weeks. Vicksburg and Port Hudson captured and
the Miss. river opened in the west. Bragg and his army
routed in the centre and Lee's army defeated in the
east. If Meade can only defeat him again, how completely great will have been our work. We are very
anxious of course about the eastern army. Every military calculation we can make demonstrates that Lee
ought to be routed, but yet it is in doubt. [John H.]
Morgan's raid in Indiana and Ohio amuses us. He can
do little harm if he escapes, and is doing much good in
arousing the people.[11] The only drawback to our good
news is the riot [12] in New York which may result in
fearful complications. If the government promptly puts
it down at any loss, we shall have no more trouble on
that score. If they do not and temporize with or suc-
cumb to the mob we might as well discontinue the war,
as our whole moral force will be lost to us. But these
questions will all be solved before this reaches you, so
there is no utility in my speculating upon them. What
we are going to do I have no idea. We are in permanent
camp, (the whole army) supplies coming up, the roads
being repaired in every direction in front, bridges being rebuilt &c., &c. Our men are drilling again, and

[11] Captured towards the end of July not far from Blennerhassett's
Island on the upper Ohio.
[12] Draft riots.

every thing looks like it did at Murfreesboro. The Pay-masters have arrived and are about paying off, and above all Gen. Rosecrans has gone to Nashville. He however has urged upon the Paymasters to use all despatch in completing their business, as he wanted his army to be ready to move as soon as possible. We are in a fine healthy location, and the whole army can move at a moment's notice. We speculate of course a great deal about our future movements, but I have re-solved them down to one of three as follows: One, to proceed on to Chattanooga and occupy that post and the Tennessee river and the concentrated railroads there, one to proceed directly east from here and move into East Tennessee. The other to move south taking Chattanooga by the way, make a juncture with Grant, and move on Mobile. But the recent victories may change all those plans. A large part of Grant's army may be thrown east to operate and we only hold the positions we have taken. But of one thing I am satis-fied. If the conscription is not stopped by mobs at home a great deal will be done somewhere in the next two months. I believe I have said almost the same thing as this in my former letters, but this is the burthen of our thoughts, planning what we will do, so naturally we talk about it. Our life here is getting monotonous again, there is nothing attractive around the country although naturally a beautiful country. But the curse of slavery here as everywhere shows itself, no improvements, no artificial beauty anywhere. With few exceptions the people poor and ignorant in fact *very* poor now, very few men of any kind to be seen now, though the male population is increasing every day, deserters from Bragg's army turning up out of the mountains all the time. We don't try to disturb them as long as they stay at their homes, without they have been particularly hard cases, from the few Union men about here we can ascertain the states of all the men about here. We have very little to amuse us except the talk of our contrabands of whom we have quite a team with us, every officer has one if not more besides laborers, teamsters, road makers, &c., &c. I was most amused yesterday at my tent-companion's man "Sam"; he has been with the Doctor for a year and of course had seen a great deal of the army. He said to the Doctor with a look of wonder: Doctor, who is dis Uncle Sam, dat you all talk about so much, de soldiers say dey are working for Uncle Sam, dat he pays um all dat he sends all dese hard bread and bacon &c. here, dat he owns all dese mules and wagons, &c. What kind of man is he? The Doctor replied gravely, that Uncle Sam was a great man north that owned the whole country and governed it &c &c. Sam listened with wonder, and said Gor-a-mighty, Doctor, how de secesh would like to get a hold of him, wouldn't dey bushwack him? then soliloquized as he walked off—"De norf must be a heep richer dan de souf, a white man here if he hab two or three hundred niggers ragged and half starved, tinks he a rich man, but just think of Uncle Sam!"

. . . You must know I feel very proud of you your letters read like those of the Roman matrons. Your patriotism has been put to the test fairly. My dearest wife for you to stand so firmly for your country, notwithstanding the personal sacrifices you are constantly making, is real cause for congratulation to me, that the one person who is all in all to me, should make me feel so proud that she was my own dear wife, causes me to be thankful indeed. Much love to all. I enclose a note to the dear children. Good-bye for the present. As ever yours

Alfred

Dechard Tenn
July 18th 1863

My Dearest Mary:

. . . We are settled down here comfortably, in a very pleasant camp, arbors around our tents, the telegraph at our very doors, and the cars will be here tomorrow. We get the night despatches before we go to bed, and I know what is going on east, twelve hours before you do. Your letter amuses me no little with your military suppositions. John Morgan's playing havoc with our rear is funny in the extreme he took especial pains to go a good ways to our rear. Gen. Rosecrans permitted him to pass us without opposition—for two reasons— He knew where he was going, and he both wanted his force away from our front, and he was willing for him to occupy our peace loving friends in our rear. We read here with intense satisfaction, of his career among the Copperheads of Indiana and Ohio for it is a truth that he has gone directly through a section thickly settled by the vermin. That though has no doubt been because he was compelled to, his intention was no doubt to march on Indianapolis, liberate the prisoners, then to Camp Chase, liberate the prisoners there, and then with an army of at least 20000 operate on our rear with a reality. But he was prevented and is only now trying to escape which I fear he will. We enjoy reading the news very much, from every section of our dear country we hear of the success of our arms, and last night the news came that the draft is progressing with no trouble except in a few localities. That in the great mob-governed City of New York even the Government is getting control. A new army to be raised, and then to look around upon *our* veterans, fit for anything, and no enemy to occupy them. Let us indeed be thankful. We can afford an occasional reverse now, we have had so much success. If Meade had only destroyed the army, the work would almost have been finished. But that will come in time. Meade will have reinforcements enough by the draft to enable him to crush the arch enemy finally. How nobly and gallantly our men have fought recently. Could men have done better? Foreign nations cannot but look upon us with surprise and admiration let them say what they will. I am especially glad to hear that the draft went off quietly in Philadelphia, and *will* take back some of my abuse of her good citizens for their want of patriotism, as they turned out at the eleventh hour, I will even believe they were not aware of their necessities before. I am anxious to hear who were drafted of my friends, you must give me a list of them as far as you hear. . . .

Business stopped me yesterday I now resume the epistle. I was struck yesterday with how little an occurrence our camp will be excited over towards evening yesterday, our whole camp was as quiet as New Berlin! When the whistle of a locomotive was heard in the distance instantly a shout went up that could have been heard for miles, and from our elevated position we could see thousands of men running like so many boys toward the railroad. What a welcome the single engine and car load got. They had just completed the bridge below Tullahoma and run down with a band of music on board. We felt considerably nearer "America" as we always call the Northern states when speaking of them.

Within a few days the road will be completed to Stevenson Station, on the Tennessee River, and then I think we will push on provided we are going that way, unless we have cavalry raids in our rear cutting the road. But if John Morgan's cavalry are captured, and Biffles [13] and Forrests detachment is removed, the Rebs, must have as much cavalry as we have by considerable. We will have good roads now, and with the railroad to bring up our supplies we can make a bold dash on Chattanooga, where Bragg is said to be now massed. We will soon have some home food to eat too. I have not tasted butter but once since leaving Murfreesboro. My meals for a week have been a regular course of fried potatoes, fried meat or ham, heavy biscuit, and tea. I am getting pretty tired of it and want a change. Gen. Rousseau is at Cowan about 6 miles from us, seven of the officers have been over to see me, among them Capt. Cummings, who I am glad to say is doing admirably; Morris does not seem very well, [Lieut. William W.] Gilbert is at Nashville sick, and [Lieut. Michael B.] Fogarty is first rate, Hays is with Genl [Absalom] Baird at Franklin. But above all Maj. [Samuel K.] Dawson is on his way down. But we will soon be rid of him. He is now the Senior Major of the Regiment and will soon be a Lt Col. and out of it. . . . Good bye and God bless you.

Alfred

Dechard Tenn July 24th 1863

My Dearest Mary:

. . . We are still quiescent here, in wondering expectation of what we are to do. And I write this extra

[13] Col. Jacob B. Biffle's regiment belonged to Brig. Gen. Nathan B. Forrest's brigade of Confederate Cavalry.

letter, because I have something important to communicate; it is this: General Rousseau sent for me yesterday, I rode over there to Cowan, six miles, and to deviate a little almost the first man I say was Maj. Dawson, walking round, looking just as usual, I did not renew our acquaintance. They received him officially at the Battalion but I am glad to say, properly, that is very coldly. But to go back to Rousseau. He has been long trying to get permission to raise 10000 mounted men for him to take command of. He now thinks he will get the permission and soon. He is to designate the officers to command them, and they are to raise the troops under his instruction, they are to be raised in different States, and the General has selected Capt. [Thomas C.] Williams and myself out of his whole command as the ones to raise and command troops from Pennsylvania. I was taken by surprise of course, and felt much honored. I never before have taken any decided step in life without consulting you, but this did not admit of the delay necessary in the case. So after some conversation I gave my consent under certain conditions, that is that my command shall be mounted infantry. Williams prefers cavalry, and there's where the hitch will be. If two regiments are to be raised there will be no difficulty, but if only one, the General may decide on cavalry; if so I shall decline. Williams is on Rousseau's staff, and I expect he has something to do in recommending me to Rousseau, but at any rate I did feel proud when Rousseau told me that he had long watched me, and that I was just one of the kind of men he wanted. I rank Williams and if the thing goes through, I shall command a regiment of mounted Pennsylvanians, and be there to raise them. Now my dear wife, all this is provided you do not object, I could not wait to ask beforehand. But if you see any good objection to it, and wish me not to I will decline; so please write to me at once, and above all *keep this a secret*. Our conversation was *strictly confidential*.

As ever your true husband,
Alfred

Dechard Tenn
July 26th 1863

My Dearest Wife:

The Sabbath has rolled around again, the usual week's routine of duty having passed without anything unusual transpiring. It is a beautiful morning and as I sit under my arbor in front of my tent I can see our soldiers taking their rest; they all have arbors, and the leaves yet green give them a picturesque appearance. Our location is very pleasant, good high ground, with a stream running near sufficiently large for bathing purposes, good drinking water from springs and wells. The sun is hot to be sure, but a fine breeze prevails all the time. I have not yet slept from under my blanket. In fact I don't believe a much more healthy location can be found. We are getting supplies of luxuries now from Nashville and are living pretty well. The cars arrive daily from above, bringing us Nashville papers of the morning, and Louisville & Cincinnati papers a day old. So we feel pretty near *America*. We have come to the conclusion that we are a fixture here for the summer which is not very satisfactory to us, notwithstanding our pleasant location; we feel as if we ought to be using these fine roads and good weather. But there is no doubt some good military reason for it, that we cannot describe. Some combinations yet to be made consequent upon the recent important military movements and successes on our side. It is very evident now that we have done all, that we originally intended to do, that is drive Bragg out of Middle Tenn and we occupy *his* fortifications. The only miscalculation that we made was, that we expected they would fight and not run, in that we were mistaken, but as our campaign was to end here, so it has to end. This is our opinion, based upon what is evident to us, that is, if we had originally intended to go further we need not have stopped here but a few days, just long enough for our supplies to come up and, the roads to dry in front. We have to thank God's mercies, that we have accomplished so much with so little loss; in fact our army is in better condition to-day if possible than when we left Murfreesboro. As I said before we feel as if we were anchored here for the summer months, but we may be mistaken, the only drawback to the argument is that all leaves, but sick leaves are refused, although "Rosy" and some of his chiefs are rusticating North. But time will reveal all, in the meantime we must enjoy to the full, and give thanks for our great successes everywhere, if we can but be permitted to capture Charleston and defeat Lee, with our present depleted army, what can we not do—with our new army after the conscripts join us? We look anxiously for news all the time from both these places, all else claims but little interest at the present time.

. . . I am so afraid I did not enjoin secrecy upon you in regard to my matters with Genl Rousseau. If not I do now, nothing was to be said about it, until the matter was decided because if the General does not get permission to raise the troops, he does not want the world to know it. He seems to be very certain he will succeed and went to Nashville yesterday about it, but I have strong doubts about it, so have not dwelt upon it much, at any rate I hope no decision will be made until I hear your decision.

I have but little mustering to do now, but the general finds some pleasant duty to occupy me continually. I notice with satisfaction, that he selects me for any delicate or confidential duty to be performed. I yesterday had a very interesting case. A Prussian who has been living in Georgia came into our lines to proceed north, having a pass from Bragg for himself and family, wife and two children, he has a protection from his own Government, Prussia. Genl. Thomas suspects that he is an emissary, and wished him examined he sent word to Genl Negley to that effect. The General directed me to attend to it with many injunctions as to the delicate nature of the business, so that no complications with his Government should arise. The joke of it is, that we only know that he is in our lines and has a pass from Bragg and his own Government's consul, he is to come here to take the cars, but we don't know his name. I examined all suspicious persons yesterday, but my friend has not arrived. I am looking anxiously for him and am bothered somewhat about examining his wife. I can take care of him well enough, but how do I know but what Mrs. Prussian has some terrible papers sewed up in her "bustle" or some such out of the way place. I wish you were here to help me, and between us may be we could fix up any important matters of that kind. But I will be very discreet, so don't be uneasy. . . . Good-bye,

As ever your true husband

Alfred

Dechard Tenn
Aug. 6th 1863

My Dearest Mary

. . . I have had another position offered me since my last which I have refused at Genl Negley's request. I have been offered a position on Genl McCook's [14] staff as Com. of Musters for the Corps; that is a higher position than I now hold as it is chief of a department in a *corps* instead of being an assistant, at the head of a division only. I submitted the matter to Genl Negley who has been very kind to me, and he frankly told me he did not want me to leave him. If it was an actual promotion, and my rank or pay was increased, he would urge me to go of course as he did in the case of Rousseau's matter, but as this did not, and only transferred me from a division to a corps, if I was personally satisfied to stay he would wish me to do so, accompanied with some complimentary remarks, saying at the same time that he had my interest at heart, and fully appreciated the services of an officer when they were properly performed and would give them the benefit of such appreciation when an opportunity occurred—his advice corresponded with my feelings and I declined the position in a polite letter thanking Genl McCook for the honor. As I know you like to hear good things said of me I will quote from the letter of [Lieut.] Col. [G. W.] Burton, who was directed by Genl McCook to offer me the position.

"Capt. Lawrence can be relieved if you accept, Rosecrans requires his successor to be named, and will be satisfied with you as the best officer in this Depart-

[14] Major General Alexander McDowell McCook was in command of the Twentieth Army Corps.

ment". I felt better satisfied after I had made my decision from receiving the congratulations of the officers of the Division that I had not left them. And Mrs. Negley (who is with us now) told me tonight when we were alone that she was very glad I had not left, as the General told her he would be very sorry if I left him, but if he thought it would advance me any he would be glad of it. Now all this is very pleasant to me, and I know it will be to you, for a proper ambition is necessary for a soldier, and I don't think I have too much of it I seek advancement and promotion as much as any body, but never have I intrigued for it nor never will I. In the absence of that advancement a just appreciation of my worth and services is a source of gratification.

A change has come over our army within the last day or two it is evident we shall move soon, I think within a week we shall start, my opinion is to Chattanooga while Burnsides makes for Cumberland Gap,—we will make a junction and occupy East Tennessee. This is my opinion only, and is based simply on the fact that Mrs. Rosecrans and other ladies at Headquarters are going to remain at Winchester. If we were going farther South, that would be no place for them, as they would be so far in the rear, a cavalry raid might make the place too hot for them. Besides Grant is evidently going to attack Mobile, and military reasons are plain that we ought to take and hold this mountain barrier. I don't know what amount of fighting we shall have but cannot see how they can present a large army at the four points attacked or threatened at once, viz: Richmond, Charleston, Mobile, and Chattanooga, leaving out the Cumberland Gap. Banks and Davidson (who I believe is the General Lewis is under) will take care of the country west of the Mississippi, with Blunt to assist them in the

Indian country. Rosecrans is great for flanking, if so he
may not have much of a fight but if he attack, we shall
have some strong fortifications to contend with. I have
no doubt it will be a hard campaign and hard living in
these mountains and valleys of East Tenn, far from our
supplies, but I would rather go there than to any other
place. This letter will reach you I think just about the
time we shall move, so you may look out for sensation
despatches. After we get off you must not expect my
letters as regular as they have been, but they will all
reach you in time, as yours will me.

As ever your true husband,

Alfred

Dechard Tenn.
Aug. 10th 1863

My Dearest Mary:

I have yours of the 3rd and cannot but feel amused
at your sanguine expectations of my coming home so
soon, and at the same time a little worried for fear you
have really learned to believe it will actually happen
and will feel the disappointment at my not so coming
if that should be. You must disabuse yourself of the
idea, I make no calculations upon it; I see by to-day's
despatches, that Rousseau is urging his idea upon the
War Dept, so you see it is not yet determined upon.[15]
And even if it is I may not be able to accept the position
for if I have to agree to *raise* a Regiment, I will not do
it, I will agree to *try* only, and some more sanguine man
than myself may promise more. So don't think too much
about it, and help me in *hoping* only. . . . We are living well now. Have corn, beans, squashes, tomatoes,

---

[15] Hough later wrote in his Autobiography that "It [the plan] fell
through however, and Rousseau returned to his old Division."

&c., so we are not suffering very terribly for our country now. But on the other side I have double duty to perform. Capt. Moody has 15 days leave of absence, and I have to perform his duties at Corps Headquarters, Genl Thomas' half a day there and the balance here, as long as we're only half a mile apart it will do well enough, but if when we move we should get some 5 or 6 miles separated, and then have field duties besides I shall have my hands full. But I do all that is put upon me without grumbling, it tells in the long run. I am not at all displeased at being with Genl Thomas for awhile, who I consider the "model soldier" so far as I have seen yet in this war. . . . And as ever my whole heart to your dear little self.

Alfred

5

* * * * * * * * *

ON AUGUST 16 the Army of the Cumberland began its movement across the Cumberland mountains, commanded by Major General William S. Rosecrans. His prized Fourteenth Army Corps was led by Major General George H. Thomas; Negley was still in command of the second division of that corps. Captain Hough noted in his autobiography that "On the 16th of August we again broke camp, moved over the Cumberland Mountains and down Crow Creek Valley without special incident, and after a few days march again went into permanent camp at Cave Spring a few miles east of Stevenson. The weather here was terribly hot, but we had a pleasant camp in a grove on a hill side. Our stay here was for the purpose of allowing the army to concentrate before pushing across the Tennessee river, as that was the obstacle between us and the enemy."

Hough described this new movement in a series of letters, the first of which is from Dechard, Tennessee. The second letter was written from Cave Spring, Alabama, the permanent camp mentioned above.

Dechard Tenn
Sunday Aug. 15th 1863

My Dearest Wife:

At last we have recommenced our movement south. I have just finished packing, and within a half an hour, we move. The order came in the night, and coming so suddenly, connected with our starting on Sunday, an unusual thing in this army, denotes something important I think. But if we are going to have active work immediately we have a long march before us to reach it as our advance is full 30 miles in front of it. . . . Trusting and hoping, believe me as ever your true and loving husband

Alfred

I send my picture the best I could get.

Headquarters 2 Div 14th A. Corps
Camp Cave Spring, Alabama
August 20th 1863

My Dearest Mary:

Thus far have we journied south. We are now only three miles from Stevenson [Alabama] on the Tennessee River, and are in camp again, where we will stay several days until the army concentrates here, Stevenson being now the Headquarters of the army. It will require several days for the army to reorganize after the march over the mountains. We have been constantly on the go since Sunday when I wrote you from Dechard. I am still very well and not at all fatigued. In fact the journey has been a delightful one. If we could only forget the sufferings of our animals over the mountain roads we could enjoy it more, but the fatigue on them is dreadful. But when I was riding ahead with the General [Negley] exploring through the forest and looking for camping ground or springs how I have enjoyed it. We arrived at this place yesterday, and went into camp this morning. Our Headquarters are on a hillside among the rocks and large forest trees, overlooking a small valley. We passed Rousseau's Division [1] about 10 miles back who had come another road a day or two before us. I saw Capt. [Thomas C.] Williams who as yet had heard nothing of our matter he had about given up all hope of it. I also saw Major Dawson [2] in the distance looking just as usual. I am happy to say he has fully sustained his reputation, since being here, which fully endorses me, for really without he had exhibited his vagaries to the officers here, it was hard to realize that what I said of him could be true. The 19th [Infantry] was on fatigue duty on this road and so when we arrived here, we found them all alone repairing a bridge. It was really delightful to meet them I had a warm reception both from the officers and the men of my company. The Band serenaded us last night, and we had a cheerful time. The country after crossing the mountains has been a long narrow valley with high mountains on both sides, very sparsely inhabited, and by the usual class of people, so nothing of interest has occurred. We expect to advance again in a few days. . . . As ever your true husband

Alfred

1 First Division, Fourteenth Army Corps, commanded until September 21 by Brigadier General Absalom Baird.

2 Dawson commanded the First Battalion, Nineteenth U. S. infantry, now a part of the Third Brigade, First division of the Fourteenth Army Corps.

Headquarters 2d Div. 14th A C
Camp Cave Springs, Ala.
Sunday Aug 23 1863.

My dearest Mary:

If you should live to be the "grandmother" you are now thinking of, I trust you will never have to experience any hotter weather than we are suffering under now. It is really terribly hot. But fortunately we are in camp and have no hard marching to do. Our Headquarters are on the mountain side, and notwithstanding the heat, are tolerable during the middle of the day and comfortable morning and evening. The nights are still cool, but there is a great difference in the temperature, between the south and north sides of the mountains, vegatation [*sic*] is much further advanced here than at Dechard, there roasting ears were just commencing, here, they are almost all too old. I fully expect we will advance again within a week as the army is almost all across the mountains and damages are nearly repaired. I hope the hot spell will be over before we march. Our pontoons are here ready for the crossing, and then ho for Chattanooga and the opening of East Tenn., Rosecrans at one end of the valley and Burnsides [3] at the other, until we meet. I suppose I shall know now very soon whether the Rousseau matter [4] will amount to anything or not, I see by the papers that he has been successful and is on his way west. That may be true or not, the papers say such monstrous stories. But if so his success may be in mounting old troops, in that case I would not be wanted. Or as is very likely "Out of sight,

[3] Major General Ambrose E. Burnside, commanding the Army of the Ohio.

[4] Rousseau was dissatisfied with only the command of a brigade and sought a higher command. C. A. Dana to E. M. Stanton, *O.R.*, Series I, Vol. XXX, pt. I, p. 220.

Alfred Lacey Hough,
about 1853

Alfred and Mary
Hough on their
wedding trip,
1857

Alfred Lacey Hough, 1861

General James S. Negley (*National Archives*)

General William S. Rosecrans (*National Archives*)

General George H. Thomas (*National Archives*)

Retreat of the Confederates from Corinth, Mississippi, and entry of the Union Army (*From a sketch by Henry Lovie. National Archives*)

Ruins of Atlanta, Georgia, 1864 (*National Archives*)

Lee and Gordon's Mills, Chickamauga battlefield, Tennessee (*National Archives*)

out of mind". He may have had to make promises to influential men to carry his point, who have *agreed* to raise men, which I would not do. So you see I don't calculate much upon the matter, anxious as I am that it will succeed. You are very facile in being willing for Williams to have [the] regiment, if I will only come home, I don't believe you, you have just as much ambition as I have, and I would be sorry if you had not. I would like to see you most dearly, but I would not make the sacrifice of my rank, or serving under an inferior, for even such a great boon as that. I know you were only joking. But oh dear how I would like to be with you and the dear little ones, if my life is spared though I think the good time is coming. If our army and navy are successful at the east, I am confident the rebellion will soon topple. We have evidence every day that they are growing weaker out here, deserters are coming to us constantly, and they all tell the same tale—Bragg will make all the resistance in his power, but he is weak, very weak, his army is dissatisfied, badly fed, badly used and disheartened. We had yesterday 11 men from one Company of Louisianians come to us, they all say that thousands would come if they dared make the attempt. Within two or three weeks I think we will be in Chattanooga, but will have to have a pretty hard fight to get it. . . . While I am writing a correspondent has just come in from Headquarters, and gives news that our cavalry have penetrated to the top of the mountain opposite Chattanooga and shelled the town, sinking two steamboats, all they had at the wharf, and causing the rebels to blow another one up they had some 20 miles down the river toward us. The rebels opened on them with cannon from 19 different points, but could not drive them off till they had completed their work. From this reconnaissance, I should judge we would move our whole force pretty soon. Deserters to-day say that [Joseph E.] Johns[t]on has superseded Bragg.[5] A Lieut-Col of the Rebels, on picket came into our lines to-day, they must be much demoralized, a vigorous fight on our part I am confident will break them down but I have no doubt they have been considerably reinforced if Johns[t]on has joined them. Our worst job will be to get across the river on our pontoons which they will oppose no doubt vigorously, we have about 40 miles yet to march before reaching Chattanooga. I intended filling this sheet, but I am called to dinner and as we have hot corn and chicken I must get close, so good bye my dearest, all love to the children. . . . I hope you got a letter after your anxiety. Good bye God bless you, as ever yours

                                        Alfred

                        Camp at Cave Springs Al
                        August 26, 1863

My Dearest Mary:

If you have not before this time, you must now divest yourself of all expectations as to my coming home. Whatever the newspapers may say about Rousseau's success, I know that it has been an utter failure. It has been no disappointment to me, as I had but little hope of his succeeding. Military reasons that were plain to me, satisfied me that he could not succeed, and my judgment has been sustained. The Government would not give him the permission to raise new troops because they thought he could not succeed, but have put him off by granting Rosecrans permission to mount Rousseau's

[5] Bragg did not relinquish his command until December 1, 1863.

old division—*which will not be done,* as it ought not to be,—it will give no additional strength to the Army and Rousseau has sent on his missive [mission] with the hope that he would increase the strength of it. So ends the matter, another ending to an ambitious expectation. I fear I am not destined to rise above a captaincy during my military career.[6] But I have the satisfaction as formerly in knowing in my own heart that I have done my duty so far. So you must continue to wait and pray for our success in redeeming East Tennessee. Our plans are maturing, and within a few days I think we will make the final advance. We will most certainly not stay in these mountain caves any longer than necessary— chills and fever abound in them, I as yet have no evidence of anything of the kind, and am taking quinine to prevent it. . . . The natives here all have the ague, a poor miserable set they are. But when we get across the river it is said to be clear of malaria. . . . I have had to buy some clothing and its horribly expensive here. Please be careful of what clothing I have and do not let it get moth eaten or damaged, at present prices my clothing bills will impoverish me. You must have my pictures by this time—poor things aint they? but I thought they would be better than none. I shall not try it again. Without you left directions at Columbia to forward your letters, you will be some time without letters from me. You did not tell me to do so but I think best to forward this and till further notice to Lewisburg. I hope our dear little ones will be well and happy during your trip. Do they grow any? What do they think about me? Do they still think that I will be back

[6] Hough retired as a colonel in 1890 and was given the rank of brigadier general, retired, in 1904. He died in 1908.

soon? And has Lacey yet the proper idea of the actual relation existing between him and his paternal parent, or does he think you are his only protector? How often I ask myself these questions and others, and how much do I think of your dear self, and wonder whether you think as I do, what we shall do and how shall we live after this "cruel war is over" if Providence should permit us to live. I begin to think it is time for me to think of it. I have never allowed myself to make any calculations for the future before, but it does really seem now as if the war was, *beginning* to draw toward the end. The rebellion is certainly growing weaker. I cannot see how we can fail in our movements here, and when successful, the shell will burst, and the people of the South will see where they stand and renounce their leaders. When the shell falls, the crash will be terrible. We have accumulating evidence daily of the demoralization of the rebel army, and the army is their sole existence, there is no government but the army, when that fails them, they are finished. The so called confederate government is merely a military despotism. One of the strongest evidences we have is the class of men deserting from them, formerly they were principally Tennesseans and Kentuckians, there were two reasons why they should desert—if they were inclined to be loyal, they wished to come into our lines, if otherwise and hated us, they wanted to protect their families from our reported depredations—in either case they were going home. Now we have Louisianians, Georgians and Alabamians coming to us, they appear to have given up all hope. One more great effort I think will tumble the whole concern to pieces. . . . Much love to all, as ever your loving husband

Alfred

Camp at Cave Springs Al
Sunday Aug 30, 1863

My Dearest Wife:

I have only time to say two things, one is that we have orders to march at once shall be off by 7 P.M. (it is near 4 P.M.) shall march all night, to Bridgeport I suppose and then cross the river. We have thrown bridges across at several places without much opposition. We take 30 days rations, you may not hear from me again for some time as we leave the railroad. Will write though as usual. . . . As ever your true husband

Alfred

On top of Raccoon Mt. south of Tennessee
River, about 10 miles, near the line between
Georgia and Alabama
Sept 4/63 8 A.M.

My Own Dearest Wife:

When I last wrote you we expected to be off in a hurry from Cave Spring, but just as we were starting, the order was countermanded, and we did not move till Tuesday noon, then pushed to the river 6 miles crossed on a pontoon bridge 1300 ft long in the night and made 6 miles that night—pushed on up the south bank of the river 18 miles next day to Morris Springs, south west from Bridgeport—pushed over this mountain[7] yester-

---

[7] "Our column crossed on an old road over Raccoon Mountain directly from Morris Springs with our Division in front. This was a heavy job, our Division was all of one day and night in ascending the Mountain, not more than two miles certainly. The work was done as follows, the Division marched till the head of the column reached the summit, and upon being well closed up, halted and stacked arms outside the road. This left a mass of men reaching from the top to the bottom of the Mountain. The artillery and trains then began to ascend, all the teams doubled, as they moved the men stationed alongside worked at the wheels, one party relieving another as the wagons moved on, the men remaining on their own ground. The ascent was

day, and here came the work. It exceeded anything I
ever saw, the very very hard work. I was left in charge
of the movement, we are all day and all night getting
the trains up the mountain only 1½ miles, we are now
all up and shall push forward down the mountain, making south west, shall strike the valley below Trenton in
Georgia, about 20 miles *south* of Chattanooga. The
General is in the front, I am in the rear with 6 orderlies,
having entire charge of the movement, reporting to him
hourly by an orderly. We have met no enemy, we are
in the front on this road, we have no news from the
rear or anywhere else, we are now fairly in Dixie, I am
full of work have important trusts placed in me and am
working with zeal and pleasure, have had no letter
from you since the 20th ult. Good bye & God bless you
and ours; as ever your true husband,

Alfred

Browns Spring Dade Co. Georgia
3 miles south of Trenton and
23 miles S W of Chattanooga
Sept 5th 1863

My Dearest Mary:

I wrote the above while on the march in hopes of
getting it off by a courier, but failed. We got into camp
here last night, and shall remain here for a day or two
to wait for the army to concentrate. We are now in
Lookout Valley, with a good road running directly to

---

finally made though we lost some wagons and several fine artillery
horses, which dropped dead in the road. We crossed the Mountain and
descended it again on the east side over the most fearfully bad roads
into Lookout Valley where we went into camp at 'Browns Spring' near
Trenton." Alfred Lacey Hough, Manuscript Autobiography, Hough
Papers.

Chattanooga, but I do not think we are going that road, but will march east, cross Lookout Mountain, and then be in a valley directly south of Chattanooga, leaving Bragg no escape south, and then with Burnside on the north of him, I think we will have him, as yet as have had no fight, much to our surprise, our advance guard have had a little skirmish on Raccoon Mountain, but it was with only a few scouts, they leave as we advance. We confidently expect a fight in crossing Lookout Mountain if the enemy do not resist us there it will be incomprehensible, as when we get across, Chattanooga will be absolutely flanked. He may count on our being obliged to retire for want of supplies, but he is mistaken, with the fresh beef and growing corn of the country of which there is plenty, we can make our supplies last 60 days—so you can imagine what a train we have and what labor we have in crossing these mountains. No army yet during this war has had the labor we have had since leaving Murfreesboro. And here we are in an Atlantic state, in good condition, as effective an army as ever entered the field. I will endeavor to give you the entire position of the different armies—take a map, and my description may enable you to make it out. Our army you know consists of 4 corps McCook on the right and the cavalry crossed Raccoon Mountain opposite Stevenson and are now below us in the same valley. We crossed opposite Stevenson Bridgeport and above, we being the advance on this road. All the Divisions are not yet over, but will be by tomorrow night, on Sunday, the entire two corps, with the cavalry, will be in this valley, the left resting on Trenton, the right some 20 miles toward Rome. [Major General Thomas L.] Crittenden's Corps I do not think has crossed the river but is immediately in front of Chattanooga. The reserve corps [Major General Gordon] Grangers holds our communication with Nashville. Burnsides as I said before is in the East Tennessee valley, north of Chattanooga. To the east of Chattanooga he is virtually surrounded. This is all I can say as to realities, the rest I can only surmize. If he finds we are crossing Lookout Mountain, I *think* he will evacuate and retire to Atlanta if he does not, and we get across without being crippled, Chattanooga with all that is in it, will be ours, in time. Now as to our march, it has been most interesting to me, I have been on important duty, having charge almost every day of the movements of the Division,—my duties have carried me along the line from front to rear frequently the incidents occurring, are so various, almost every phase of character, and disposition is exhibited by the men, and the vagaries of the mules add not a little to the variety. What labor I have seen performed, and how cheerfully it has been done, I have seen 19 mules pulling and all the men that could get room pushing, to get up some places, and yet we have brought over about 250 wagons including the artillery, that is of our Division alone. And then the scenery you have never seen any thing equal to the views in some places, but I cannot describe it. I did wish for you so many times, the pleasure would have been great to you. The inhabitants are very few and with few exceptions very ignorant most of the men are in the army, or hiding in the mountains, afraid to go to the army and equally afraid of the Yankees. Our movement over here has very much surprised them, they did not see how we could cross the river after they had burnt the bridge. But I must close. . .

Alfred

Sept. 13th 1863 [8]
At Stevens Gap on Top of Lookout Mt
My dearest Mary

I wrote you a note last night which is just now about leaving, and being at this moment on duty as "Signal officer" on top of the mountain right over our camp, which lies about 400 feet immediately beneath us and

[8] See the Report of Major General James S. Negley of September 17, 1863, for the activities of the Second Division, Fourteenth Army Corps from September 1 to 13. *O.R.* Series I, Vol. 30, pt. I, pp. 324-328. Hough himself later gave an account of his activities between the dates of September 5 and 13.

"After a short stay here [Brown's Spring] we moved across Lookout Valley and began to ascend Lookout Mountain about, I should think 16 miles south of Chattanooga. At the crest of the Mountain are palisades with a steep winding road to pass through them, this road was barricaded by the enemy and a heavy stone breast work was built across the only gap to be seen for miles. At this place about 100 mounted men barred our passage for a whole day. Several attempts were made to dislodge them, but all were repulsed. That night a Union man came into camp and offered to lead a column by a secret path to the top, a regiment was sent with him, and by difficult climbing up a narrow pathway they reached the top, about three miles from the road we were on. Taking the enemy in the rear in the early morning the road was soon cleared, the enemy galloping off across the Mountain and down the other side without firing another shot. They had done us much damage however before this was done. We then moved across the top of the Mountain and down the other side through Stevens Gap into McLemores Cove without difficulty, the only incident I noted at the time on the Mountain was finding plenty of watermelons and I am certain they were never more grateful to me than they were then. We also found plenty of green corn here which we had missed for some time before, it being rather too late for it in the Cumberlands.

"We left our camp at Stevens Gap on the 10th of Sept and pushed on to Baileys cross roads about 4 miles, on the 11th we pushed boldly on towards Lafayette where the enemy were said to be. Our crossing the Mountains had flanked Chattanooga causing it to be evacuated, the enemy moving down the Atlanta R. R. Thomas's Corps was all crossing Lookout Mountain at and near where we were. McCooks the same further south, and Crittendens had crossed at Chattanooga after its evacuation and were in possession.

"There has been much discussion about movements here, but my opinion after the judgement of years is that we supposed the enemy were in full retreat and our object was to intercept them, but we were

seeing nothing to communicate, I fill the time by writing
this to send the first opportunity. As I predicted in my
last, we pushed on over the mountain having slight
fighting all the way over, McCook crossing at the same
time some 12 to 20 miles south of us, Crittenden, bearing directly on Chattanooga, our crossing flanked Chat-

---

mistaken, their intention was to drive us out and cut us off in detail.
With this preface I will proceed. We moved on from Baileys Cross
Roads and had no difficulty till we neared the hills across McLemores
Cove where upon crossing a bridge we were compelled to dislodge a
battery and at a stream beyond, infantry behind a stone wall gave us
some trouble. But until we reached a gap debouching from Pigeon
Mountain we were not held in check. Here while attempting to force
our way through at Dug Gap it was discovered that the enemy were
pouring over Pigeon Mountain on both our flanks. Genl. Negley decided
to retreat at once previously sending to Genl. Thomas for assistance,
who sent Genl. Bairds Division, (Rousseau's, who was in Washington yet). The Division was formed into two lines with heavy flanking columns, and the retreat began, the 3rd Brigade we left in position facing the enemy, while the rest marched on to the hill we had
crossed and there formed line of battle. I was left in charge of the
3rd Brigade with instructions to keep our position till the enemy
struck us, then to resist sharply till they were checked, and then retreat
rapidly through the line to the rear, now our front. All this was done,
we gave one volley along the whole line as the cavalry struck us, they
were evidently surprised at our action and fell back with many empty
saddles. We retreated at double time previously having placed a Regt.
behind the stone wall before spoken of, we got through the 2nd line
before the enemy again reached us, though we could hear sharp firing
on both our flanks. The Regiment behind the stone wall gave one volley
and then double quicked up the hill and followed us. The 2nd line
remained on the hill till after a sharp fight and then retreated through
us, we having formed a line on the next rising ground to the rear. In
this manner the retreat was conducted, till we met Bairds Division, we
then made a stand and held the enemy in check till our retreat was
made safe to Stevens Gap which we reached after dark tired and
weary. We lost only 48 men in this affair, and not a wagon or animal
though our whole train was with us.

"We afterwards learned that we had a narrow escape, and that the
Officer in command of the enemy, Genl. [Thomas C.] Hindman was
much blamed for not capturing us, as he had a largely superior force.
General Negleys decision to retreat in the affair was determined in a
great measure by two incidents which came to my notice. One was the
conduct of a rebel Officer a young Lieutenant whom we captured on
the picket line. He was so defiant in his manner and boasted so loudly

tanooga, and the enemy evacuated it, but to prevent our
cutting off their retreat they pushed on down in force to
cut us off in detail while separated. Our Division being
in advance, after we left this camp three days since, they
pushed over Pigeon Mountain (the only mountain sep-
arating us from their railroad) and completely envel-
oped us we discovered it in time however, and commenced our retreat to this camp again. Rousseau's
(now Baird's) Division came up to us just in time, having crossed the mountain in the night to our relief.[9]
We had a most exciting time, but the retreat was con-

---

that we would have our hands full before we got through the ridge
that the General was led to suspect what really proved to be the
truth in regard to the enemy. The other was a conversation with a
small boy who wandered into our lines, a talk with him brought out
the fact that the body of the enemy were then at his home about a mile
from us and on our flank, the boy told it very innocently with no idea
that he was giving valuable information. This action and other dis-
coveries changed the position of affairs and General Rosecrans saw
that instead of pursuing what he supposed was a flying enemy, he
must concentrate for a battle to save Chattanooga, he knew now that
the enemy had been reinforced by troops from the East.

"I am aware that some historians have endeavored to show that the
original object only was to get into Chattanooga and that the battle of
Chickamauga was necessary to accomplish this, but I am positive there
was no such idea at that time. I was present at a conversation between
Genl. Rosecrans and some of his Officers the next morning after the
Dug Gap affair and heard with pain that the weight of opinions
among them was that no enemy in force would be found in our front.
They doubted the reports of Negley and Baird and seemed to think
they had been unnecessarily frightened. The events of that day how-
ever satisfied them for the enemy were found at several points."
Alfred Lacey Hough, Manuscript Autobiography.

[9] On the 10th [of September] Negley's division advanced to within
a mile of Dug Gap, which he found heavily obstructed, and Baird's
division came up to his support on the morning of the 11th. Negley became satisfied that the enemy was advancing upon him, in heavy force,
and perceiving that if he accepted battle in that position he would
probably be cut off, he fell back after a sharp skirmish, in which
General Baird's division participated, skillfully covering and securing
their trains, to a strong position in front of Stevens Gap." Report of
Major General William S. Rosecrans, October, 1863, *O.R.*, Series I,
Vol. XXX, Part I, 54.

ducted in a most masterly manner. Genl Negley has
stamped his character as military man by this affair
even if it had not been established before. We did not
lose a wagon, horse or gun, our killed and wounded will
reach nearly 50, but there is much more, one ambuscade
of behind a stone wall which we left to meet them as
they came up after our forces had fallen back dropped
about 40 of them, they came up cheering thinking we
were all on the next hill, but their cheering suddenly
turned to wailing, and in the confusion one party two
companies of the 19th Ill, made good their retreat to us
without a scratch. Our artillery then opened on that
point doing terrible havoc, while we were doing this,
other of our troops had been placed in position protecting both of our flanks, they attacked both flanks in
every available place but were signally repulsed, they
even got cavalry (a small body) in our extreme rear,
within a mile of our present camp, but we had troops
there in time to drive them out, meanwhile our trains
were quickly pushing their way through the centre of
our lines, and as we neared home our rear guard gradually grew stronger from the flanking troops being relieved, and at 10 o'clock at night I threw myself down
on my cot tired and exhausted, yesterday I rested and
to-day I am as fine as silk. I had the satisfaction yesterday, upon saying Good morning to Genl Negley of having him tapping me on the shoulder smiling at the time,
saying Good morning Captain; you had the honor of
conducting the rear guard last night and indeed I never
felt greater relief in my life than when I sent an orderly
to Genl Negley to report to him that I was up with the
3d Brigade Several times I was in the midst of very hot
fire, but none of their shells came near me, musket balls
were very frequent and very close, but none harmed me.

I will never forget that position of ours, at the stone wall, and the hill this side of it on which we were posted and from which we poured in our shells upon them. For in the very same place on the day before they caught us. I had charge of the advance and was immediately behind the skirmishers as our men rose the hill, one some 20 feet in advance cried "Down boys", we all "downed" and the bullets whistled over our heads, they were from behind the stone wall.

In Camp an hour later.

I was suddenly stopped with my letter, by a signal to come down, and here I am, but I must tell you about my being a signal officer. For some reason or other, we have no signal officers with us, at the very time they would be of great use. So I was sent up on the mountain this morning to see what I could and was to signal with a code of my own invention, but it did not work well, that is all of it, as the signal to come down was for them at the camp to hold the flag straight up, but unfortunately they forget, and were only standing still resting and forgot that the flag was standing up. So I took it for a signal and down I came. We have had quite a laugh over it. I find the Generals of Divisions and Genl Thomas in consultation. They don't know whether to advance or not and are I believe waiting for information. If we could get Bragg's army in a position where our whole army could concentrate we would fight him, but he will not fight. I was in hopes Chattanooga would end our campaign, but am now afraid we will have to go to Atlanta. I cannot begin to tell you of our work, but if I live it will be long a subject of conversation. From all accounts it is decidedly the hardest campaign of the war. You must recollect, that we are travelling over mountains and have to carry *all* of our provisions, there is nothing to eat in the country. But it will be easier now as they can soon bring by rail to Chattanooga, and there are no mountains between us and there. I suppose you will be glad to hear of the occupation of Knoxville and Chattanooga, thereby giving us East Tennessee, but their army is still in existence, and it is our duty to follow it until it is destroyed, and that may be yet through a deal of hard work. But I am still living and well by the blessing of God. . . . God bless you and ours.

Alfred

In Camp at Birds Mills
Walker Co., Georgia
Sept 18th 1863

My Dearest Wife

I again have an opportunity of writing to you, although my desk is a book upon my knees, and the occasional report of cannon on our left flank, reminds me that I may have to stop at a moment's notice, and call for horse and sword. In my last I told you of our retreat to Stevens Gap. Since then, we have ascertained that our escape was almost miraculous, they were six to our one, but we were preserved with the loss of 18 killed and wounded, and no loss of transportation, which is the real substance of our existence.—But our discovery of the enemy was of importance, as it discerned to Genl Rosecrans that they were prepared to fight him, and it behooved him to get into position to receive them as quick as possible, as his army was separated, and no one part of it strong enough to receive battles from the combined forces of the enemy. Further developments demonstrated that they had received large reinforcements besides [Simon B.] Buckner's

Corps,[10] which Burnsides had driven out of East Tennessee, [Joseph E.] Johns[t]on has sent him a corps or two Divisions, and finally [James] Longstreet's Corps is just joining him from the Richmond army. Altogether they considerably outnumber us. But we have worked night and day, and this morning I am happy to say we are in line of battle ready to receive them if they attack us, and in position to take such measures and plans to attack them if we choose to do so. But I have no idea we will make the attack unless we get reinforcements, it would be folly to do so, as they outnumber us, and have the advantage of position. Our line extends along the north side of Chickamauga Creek, running from N E to S W, we are near the centre and about 16 miles from Chattanooga. The enemy's position is in and about Lafayette, a spur of Pigeon Mountain lying between us, a series of hills which they have possession of—a strong position, which we must drive them out of before we can advance upon them. There has been skirmishing along our whole line during our movement to get into position, and even yet they are feeling of us at all points, and as I write at this moment, the firing of artillery is quite sharp towards our left, which may possibly be the beginning of a battle. To sum up the matter I have reason to believe that reinforcements must be sent us or we cannot advance any further, and if they should attack us here the advantage would be on their side this is not a very hopeful view of the matter, but then we have Chattanooga to fall back upon, and prepare for another campaign. This battle is of all importance to the rebels, hence their immense efforts to prevent a defeat. If they should be defeated, the rebellion is virtually ended in the southwest. Hence also the

[10] Third Corps, Army of Tennessee.

importance of our defeating them, and of our having strength enough to do so. The government is fully aware of our position as Genl [Henry W.] Halleck telegraphed that Longstreet Corps had left the Richmond Army fully confirming the reports of deserters before.

I have never as fully realized the iniquity of this rebellion as I have since crossing the Tennessee River. The so called government is only a military despotism the people or rather the majority of them in this section are staunch Unionists, though the sons and brothers of many of them are in the rebel army, forced into the ranks to fight against what they believe to be right. We have discovered many a patriot-hero among these people who have made terrible sacrifices for their opinions, and how gladly we have been welcomed by them, oh how my blood has boiled to hear some of the stories of their sufferings. I trust in our merciful Father that you may never have to undergo the sufferings of these people.

Well my dearest before this reaches you we may have had a great battle, and the appearances are that there will be one. I must close as order has just come to get into line, if we fight I may not finish this, if not in due time I will, may God bless you and ours and preserve me to meet you again. With all love and affection, your husband

Alfred

Chattanooga Sept 23 1863
7 o'clock P M

My Dearest Wife:

I am safe and well after a most terrible battle, and it does seem hard that I cannot even have an opportunity to sit down and write to you as fully as my heart dictates. But it cannot be done. For six days and nights I have not eaten a regular meal, or had a regular sleep, but taken food and rest just as I could get it, and but little rest have I had. I write this in my order book while at work, and will only say that we were attacked by Bragg by overpowering numbers, when we were not ready for it, and were defeated, our loss was great as was theirs also but we have fallen back to here, and are fortifying night and day, I am busy as an engineer. If Bragg had followed us he could have ruined us, he has given us two days to fortify and now I think he cannot whip us. They are now in front, and if they attack it will be tomorrow, if they do not, they will then try to flank and compel us to evacuate, reinforcements for us are on the way, and if they come, they can prevent the flank movement but if they do not and we have to fall back, the whole campaign is a failure. So ends the story I will write you a history of the battle when I can, but now I will only say that it was terrible.[11] I did not expect to live through it, and oh how I thought of you and my dear ones, but God was merciful, and I still live, as Jesse has expressed it I was outwardly calm I did my duty *well* My dearest we are to have more battles, I trust I shall still be preserved most likely you will hear by telegraph of one before this reaches you Jesse telegraphed you that I was safe, I hope he can do so again. I must close and attend to my business. The men are working on the fortifications, and are as cheerful and confident as ever, they are in great spirits. With all love for all of you I am as ever yours,

Alfred

[11] See Captain Hough's report of the battle of Chickamauga in the *Official Records,* Series I, Vol. 30, pt. I, pp. 346-350.

Hough's letter of September 18, written in a speculative vein before the anticipated battle, was followed by the letter of September 23 which related, in a telegraphic way, that he had been through a terrible ordeal. This last letter gives few details. The writer was exhausted from his continuous excitement and lack of sleep; his principal desire was to reassure his wife that he was safe. Some years later, from notes and excerpts of his letters, the veteran of Chickamauga reconstructed the events of those fatal September days in his autobiography.

"For some days the whole army was concentrating and finally on the 18th we were on the west bank of Chickamauga Creek, the enemy opposite to us, the struggle was near at hand. Our Division was in camp at Owens Ford on the 18th, and just before night it was ordered to move to the left and relieve [Major General John M.] Palmers [2nd] Division of Crittendens Corps [Twenty First] in the neighborhood of Crawfish Springs, where Genl. Rosecrans Head Quarters were. We were soon on the march but there being a difficulty about orders to Palmer to be relieved, that are too tedious to explain, there was a delay in effecting the movement, and it was not completed till midnight. I will only say that I was not out of the saddle till near 2 o'clock in the morning, and conducted one of the Brigades to the front to relieve one of Palmers (Gross's), and had to do it under fire, a constant picket firing being kept up. During that night there was a continued movement from our right to our left, and morning found our Division on the extreme right of the advanced front excepting some cavalry to the right of us, the remainder of Genl. Thomas's Corps next on the left. We had desultory fighting in front of us that morning, but we could hear [a] fierce battle raging to our left.

"About 11 o'clock A.M. an order came for Genl Negley to move to the left and take order [*sic*] from Genl. McCook whose Corps was next to us. We withdrew from line and were soon in column moving quickly, passing through many wounded going to the rear and suffering some from stray shells falling in our midst, but before we could get into position under McCook another order came for us to keep right on and join Genl. Thomas on [his?] left as speedily as possible. Genl. Rosecrans Head Quarters were now at the Widow Glens house farther to the left, and as we passed it, he came out and pointing to the front and left, said to Genl. Negley 'You will find the enemy right on there.' I returned to Negley with the message and we formed line of battle with one Brigade (Beatty's) in reserve and marched to the front. We pushed forward some distance, the advance of the enemy falling back. This ground had been fought over in the morning and we had to march over the bodies of friend and foe alike, now cold and stiff in death; it was a sad spectacle but we moved stolidly on.

"At last we reached the enemy in line who delivered their first fire in a volley and for half an hour we had a fierce fight along our whole line. We struck them just after sunset and their first volley showed a sheet of fire that lighted them up so that I could see their faces. This volley so frightened my horse that he reared and threw me, but I kept on on foot, my horse running to the rear. Fortunately he went to our Division Hospital and I recovered him next morning. Our fight was soon over; we were victorious; this was the last struggle of consequence on that day [the 19th]. After the enemy had fallen back we joined the main line of battle a little to the rear and laid on our arms for the night. I had but little rest that night for after being relieved from duty it was too cold to sleep, so, especialy as I had lost my blankets with my horse, I went to a camp fire somewhat to the rear and went soundly to sleep along side it, but after I got to sleep some straggling soldier rolled me away from the fire and laid down in my place. I awoke nearly perished with cold, and notwithstanding I did for the soldier what he had done for me, I slept no more as it was soon daylight.

"That night General Negley received orders that he would be relieved early in the morning by [Maj.] Genl. [Thomas J.] Woods Division [12] and that he would go on to Genl. Thomas who was still on the extreme left, while we were still to the right of center. Here another blunder occurred somewhere and we were not relieved till near noon, though messengers were constantly coming from Genl. Thomas for us to hurry. We had only desultory firing on our front this morning [September 20] but no regular charge. Finally we were relieved by Wood, and we immediately began our march of two Brigades along the rear of the line of battle, the reserve Brigade having been sent to Genl. Thomas some time before. We moved at double time directly in the rear of the line now fighting and it was virtually through a storm of missiles, we being on higher ground than the troops in combat between us. Here the after troubles of Genl. Negley began, for he never reached Genl. Thomas, but in obedience to an order he said he received from one of Genl. Thomas's staff officers, Capt. Gaw, and have no doubt he did, he

[12] First Division of Crittenden's Twenty-first Army Corps.

stopped and took a position on a hill, where were a number of batteries and parts of batteries. It is denied that such an order Genl. Negley said he received was ever given. While he was getting into position, the crash came and the whole right of our army gave way, all on the right of us appeared to be falling to the rear with the debris of the right of the army, and had apparently given up the fight. Upon my return, bye the bye, I could not go over the same ground I had gone over as it was then in the possession of the enemy, I found Genl. Negley marching his command to the rear. This act was the cause of his after trouble, but as it was done during my absence in search of Genl. Rosecrans I cannot form an opinion as to whether he was justified in doing it or not. I only know that up to that time no act of his in the battle or before it could be questioned.

"Negley fell back to MacFarlands Gap, directly to the rear of the battle ground; there he met Generals Sheridan and Jeff C. Davis the Division Commanders whose commands had given way on the right. They now heard that all was not lost, that although Genl. Rosecrans and two of his Corps Commanders, McCook and Crittenden had given up and gone to Chattanooga, Genl. Thomas with his own (excepting Negley) and parts of the other two Corps and the reserves under Granger was still holding his ground and intended to. I was deeply interested during the interview between these officers, at which also Col. [Arthur Charles] Ducat, Rosecrans Inspector General, was present, but they could come to no agreement for common action. After a conversation they each decided to go to Genl. Thomas independently, but the day was far spent, and night came on before any of them reached him. Negley, intending to go to Thomas, left in the wake of Sheridan,

but some time after him and only reached Rossville in
a gap in Missionary Ridge to the rear of the battle field.
Here night fell upon him and he stopped. If he had kept
on and followed Sheridan who almost reached Thomas,
I have no doubt he would have saved himself, but his
stopping there left a doubt upon his intentions. Most of
the army reached Rossville before morning as Genl.
Thomas retreated under cover of darkness often resist-
ing charge after charge of the enemy, he there most
bravely earned his title of the 'Rock of Chickamauga.'

"About 10 o'clock at night before General Thomas
arrived the confusion and disorder was great at Rossville, the retreating troops seeing others here stopped,
and being tired and worn out threw themselves down
anywhere, there was no head to, no order in, the mass.
I truly believe that a charge of one Regiment of
Cavalry suddenly made would have routed the whole
mass, but thanks to General Thomas they were kept too
busily occupied for any such movement.

"The confusion and disorder being so great General Negley sent me to Chattanooga to report the facts
to Genl. Rosecrans, and ask for instructions as to what
to do under the circumstances. I took a horse (my third
one so far in the battle) and rode the six miles, following the main road through the dark according to directions received, and after some difficulty found General
Rosecrans about midnight in the telegraph office in the
act of telegraphing Washington. He looked worn and
exhausted and was laboring under excitement, he heard
my statement but in doing so showed the want of one
requisite of a great military commander, firmness and
self reliance under adverse circumstances. He was evidently crushed under the weight of his disaster; skill-
ful, energetic, and brave, his nervous temperament

overbalanced all and exposed his one weakness.[13] He
told me to return with all haste and tell General Negley
to preserve order till Genl. Thomas reached him, or
Thomas should retire to Rossville and the whole army
under him would make a stand there. I rode back
wearily and on reaching there found General Thomas
with the troops that had remained with him all there
and most of them sleeping soundly where they had
halted. After reporting I was dismissed for the night,
tired, sleepy and hungry, wondering where I could find
something to eat, when to my surprise and amazement
my faithful John Thomas presented himself to me
with a haversack full of substantials."

With the appearance of food, and the prospect of
rest, Captain Hough's morale took a turn for the better as the battle of Chickamauga ended. After a night's
sleep, he spent the following day "loaned" to General
Rousseau who was rounding up stragglers after the
battle. When night came the retreat to Chattanooga
began, after a breastworks had been thrown up as a
ruse to make the enemy think that the battle was to be
rejoined. "The march that night was most impressive,"

13 Judge Charles M. Hough, the son of Alfred Lacey Hough, has left
a comment on Rosecrans which he heard from his father. "The scene
which only once he told me of, as illustrative of the unwisdom with
which armies may be led, he beheld at the close of Chickamauga's second day. His Brigade Commander sent him from far on the right wing
to find Headquarters, find Rosecrans, find someone who could and
would give orders for that Brigade had fought all day without them.
By night Capt. Hough rode miles toward and almost into Chattanooga,
until he found the house in which General Rosecrans was, and discovered him crying, despairing, and even seeking spiritual comfort
from the priest who was his confessor and formed part of his body-
guard. Orders from the Commander there were none, and my father
rode back with the advice of some minor Generals whom he met there
'to close in on the center;' and with that Brig. Gen. Negley had to be
content." Marginal note by Charles M. Hough in the manuscript copy
of the Autobiography of Alfred Lacey Hough.

Hough later wrote, "it reminded me much of the description in Irvings Life of Washington of the evacuation of Long Island by our troops during the Revolutionary War. In passing the column I did not hear a word from a man, I had some difficulty in picking my way on the road side past them, I did finally reach the head of the Division and joined Genl. Negley just out of Chattanooga; the rear of the Division came in just before daybreak." The battle of Chickamauga was over, the federal forces had retreated to Chattanooga, and the tired Captain managed to find a bed in quarters of his brother-in-law, Jesse Merrill, who was at Rosecrans' headquarters. In a few moments he was fast asleep.

Sept. 25 1863

I put this in my desk in a hurry previous to going into battle. My desk was opened to-day for the first time, and I forward you the letter. I am surprised at the correctness of my views. I only reiterate now what I said then, we must have reinforcements. We are in the same relative position, we were before the battle. Our losses being about equal.

Affectionately,

Alfred

Chattanooga Oct 3 1863

My Dearest Wife:

I sent you a letter day before yesterday, we have every reason to suppose its gobbled up by the rebels. They have made no attack on our front yet, but their cavalry are trying to cut off our communication, and yesterday morning destroyed part of one of our trains, among which I suppose was my letter, but it may possibly have got through. I suppose you will hear of another scare in Kentucky now, as part of them have gone there I understand. Our reinforcements are close by, and, our communications our one weak point. If they can cut off our supplies, they will hurt us badly,—I do wish things would come to a crisis, this suspense is terribly wearing. To live, and go to sleep knowing that a hundred or so of cannon are looking one another in the face, and may at any moment open on each other, that is our daily life, but it *must* soon end, a fight or a fall back by one side or the other must take place before many days. I am still very well, and busy. I have not time to write a letter now, as I send this by a private messenger and he is waiting. Love to all, to the dear children, and my whole heart for you. . . .

Alfred

6

* * * * * * * * *

AFTER HIS LETTER HOME on October 3, Hough did not write again for over two weeks. In the meantime, as he related in his subsequent memoirs, the Army of the Cumberland underwent considerable change and his own career was affected by developments. He was particularly upset at his separation from Negley. His later writing reveals the situation more clearly than his letters.

"By severe labor Chattanooga was soon in condition to hold out against the enemy, but our line of supplies was broken and held by the enemy, and we looked forward to a starving time till aid should open up the road to us.

"Soon after we had become fairly fixed in Chattanooga great changes took place in the Army which seriously affected me. As is always the case somebody must be held responsible for misfortunes, so the Army was reorganized, a number of General Officers were relieved and among them Genl. Negley; his division was broken up and soon after Genl. Thomas relieved Genl. Rosecrans. The justice of removing Genl. Negley I will not discuss, he certainly was most unfortunate before the close of the battle when he left his position, but under the condition of affairs and as he saw them, I must hold him blameless, at least intentionally so. Genl. Thomas has told me since that he could not understand it, Negley had been such a reliable man before, and always had such a good Division, and kept it so well in hand, that he could not understand how he could have failed him so on that day.

"However the changes were made, the Division broken up, and I was transferred to Head Quarters of the Army as an assistant to the Chief Commissary of Musters of the Dept; this brought me on to the staff of Maj. General Thomas though in a minor position. I was much grieved at the change for I knew it would deprive me of prominence in field duty, and this I had learned to like and feel that I was well fitted for; it proved however to be to my personal advantage in the end as will be shown. My duties now brought me close to Genl. Thomas; Capt. Young the Chief Commissary of the Dept. remained at Nashville where the permanent Head Quarters of the Dept. were, and I represented him with the General in the field, and thus I was installed at Head Quarters with Genl. Thomas whom I never left except temporarily till death separated us.

"My duties now were entirely in the office but they required constant attention, so many questions of law and of orders, arose during the re-enlistment of the Veteran Volunteers at this time, that I had to study much to be prepared to meet them, and much work was necessary in my department to effect their proper organization."

Headquarters Department of the Cumberland,
Office Commissary of Musters
Chattanooga Oct. 18 1863

My dearest Mary

After long delay I have two letters from you, Sept. 28th and Oct. 3d the former from Danville and the latter from Lewisburg. . . . I have been dreadfully homesick since Genl Negley left. I felt as if I *must* go with him, and the disappointment was hard to bear. This feeling was intensified, because I felt that my usefulness would be much greater with him than in any position I shall have here now. But I have overcome it, and have settled down to work in my new position, without the least hope of seeing you for a long long time. Genl. Negley will endeavor to have me report to him through an order from the War Department, but the objections here are so strong that I have not the least hope of it, unless you can get some influential friend to accomplish it. My position is A. C. Musters at Dept Headquarters, being 2nd to Capt [John H.] Young, Chief Mustering officer of the Dept. The duties are light and pleasant, and what will be pleasant news to you I suppose, take me entirely from field duty, hence my feeling, of non-usefulness, for in the field I feel my own worth, and know that I am doing good. . . . And our daily life here is a history, that can never be written. Here are two armies facing each other, in full view of each other not two miles apart, their pickets within a quarter of a mile of each other, meet daily and exchange papers, have friendly chats, no firing at each other. While the main armies are both preparing for a deadly conflict, one getting heavy guns in position in readiness to shell, and burn their opposers, while the cavalry are attacking in the rear, and the other, fortifying to resist the attack, for the first few days after we were in here, they attempted to shell us out, but they produced no effect and desisted, they are now evidently throwing up works preparatory to getting heavier guns in position, but we are working like beavers and in time this place will be well fortified, we also are getting heavy guns. Their cavalry raid appears to be stopped, they did us considerable damage though, and we are now short of rations, the poor horses, how they suffer, many die daily. If I had been suddenly thrown from the comforts of home, and the scenes of prosperity around me into such a place as this I should have thought it horrible, very horrible, but we have become used to it, we are as cheerful and as happy as you are, *only* when we think of home, then oh then how our hearts sicken. Hooker now covers our communications, and I suppose a large army will concentrate here as soon as supplies can be brought up.[1] A great battle will be fought here or near here but how soon I cannot say. If they attack us here the fight will be terrible, I do not *think* they could drive us out now, and in a short time all

[1] Thomas, in his report to the Committee on the Conduct of the war outlined the position of the Army of the Cumberland at this particular time: "The Department and Army of the Cumberland at that time comprised the following commands: the Fourth and Fourteenth army corps, at Chattanooga, three divisions of cavalry, the local garrisons of Middle Tennessee, and the Eleventh and Twelfth army corps under command of Major-General Joseph Hooker, just arrived from the East, whence they had been despatched to reenforce the army at Chattanooga, and which were, at the time . . . guarding the railroad from Bridgeport to Nashville. The forces at Chattanooga were in a very precarious condition from the difficulty of obtaining supplies, the only means of procuring which was by wagons and over sixty miles of almost impassable mountain roads, the enemy holding the river and the railroad between Chattanooga and Bridgeport; and his cavalry had destroyed one large train laden with supplies, numbering over three hundred wagons, on its way from Bridgeport to Chattanooga. The question of holding Chattanooga was then simply that of supplies." Quoted by Van Horne, p. 154.

the force they can bring cannot do it. And if we once get fortified and provisioned, we can resume the offensive again but that will [be] a long time yet. . . . ever your loving husband

Alfred

Headquarters Dept of Cumb
Chattanooga Oct 20 1863

My Dearest Wife:

. . . I am fairly domiciled here at Headquarters. Capt Young the chief commissary goes to Nashville, and I remain at Headquarters, as A C M for the Dept. That is I represent him in the field and am a general supt of mustering of the troops in the front, and have a house for an officer. Am very well, also Jesse.[2] We are undergoing a change of Commanders to-day, Genl Rosecrans goes I don't know where, and Genl Thomas takes command. The change somewhat astonished the Army, but I cannot say that I was surprised. It has been evident to me for a long time that Genl Thomas would eventually command this Army.[3] Anyhow, the efficacy of the Army will not be injured by the change. . . . In haste your loving husband

Alfred

[2] Captain Jesse Merrill, brother of Mrs. Hough, was Chief Signal Officer, Army of the Cumberland.

[3] In a dispatch dated September 30, 1863, Edwin M. Stanton had advised the Assistant Secretary of War, C. A. Dana, that "all the Army of the Cumberland can need will be a competent commander. The merits of General Thomas and the debt of gratitude the Nation owes to his valor and skill, are fully appreciated here; and I wish you to tell him so. It is not my fault that he was not in chief command months ago." On October 16, 1863, in General Order No. 337, which appointed U. S. Grant to command the Division of the Mississippi, Thomas succeeded Rosecrans. He formally assumed command of the Army of the Cumberland on October 20. Thomas B. Van Horne, *The Life of Major General George H. Thomas,* New York, 1882, p. 152.

Head-quarters Department of the Cumberland,
Office Commissary of Musters
Chattanooga Oct. 22 1863
My Dearest Mary:

It still rains, in vain we look for the clear sky, every day we feel more and more cut off from home. The roads now are almost impassable. I understand we have about 12 days rations ahead only, and our horses have been sent to the rear for want of forage, and if the roads do not get better by that time, we must starve or fall back. But we trust in Providence, that we shall be preserved from so dire a calamity. You may rest assured we shall not fall back if we can avoid it. To do so would be to give up all we have given so much blood and treasure for. The enemy have apparently given up the idea of assaulting us from the front. They show no sign of so doing, if they should we are well prepared for them, and in the meantime we are building an interior line of permanent fortifications that could be held by a small force. Their plan is to cut off our communications and flank us.[4] And at the present time while they keep a sufficient force in front of us, I think they are moving on Burnsides [*sic*] to push him back and get into our rear, Hooker being too strong to push back, I trust Burnsides [*sic*] can hold his own. If we only had clear weather and good roads, I should have no fear,

[4] "Bragg, now that Chattanooga could not be occupied without a contest, could think of nothing more enterprising than to establish his army in a position of quasi-investment, spread out in a semicircle some six miles long. His left reached to the foot of Lookout Mountain, where the railroad from Chattanooga to Bridgeport squeezed between the mountain and the river, and cut Rosecrans off from rail connection with his base at Nashville. The Confederate line extended eastward across Chattanooga Creek to Missionary Ridge, and along the north face of the ridge to Chickamauga Creek about two miles from its confluence with the Tennessee above the city." Stanley F. Horn, *The Army of Tennessee,* Indianapolis, 1942, p. 281.

but we cannot contend against the elements. We hear
they are fighting on the Potomac, but have faith that
Meade can hold them where they are, and that is all
that is wanted. This war now is merely a question of
which side will become exhausted first, and if our people at home will only sustain us by *means* we have no
fear of the result. In our department (the mustering)
we are just commencing the organization of veteran
volunteers, and from appearances we shall be successful
to a great degree,—what a fine army that will be,
picked men from this already army of veterans. You
would be astonished to see how our men have learned
to take care of themselves. They all have houses, built
of boards, sticks, bricks, stones, mud, in fact of almost
everything. And to see what discipline has done for
them; I myself was surprised to see how little the
change of Commanders affected them, you would not
have known it from seeing or hearing anything unusual.
I enclose the orders of both Generals—they are notable
for brevity. Our Grand Commander Genl Grant is
expected here daily [5]—you may not understand that
Grant now commands all the Western Armies, Genl
Thomas being under him. The Departments of Ohio,
Cumberland & Tennessee being in the Grand Division
of the Mississippi under the command of Grant. This
is I think a good arrangement, as they can now work in
concert and not at cross purposes as formerly.

We are much gratified here at the election news, and
hope now that the Government will not be afraid to
call upon the people to push on the war. I still keep
very well, am still in a tent though, but hope to get in
a house as soon as Capt Young leaves, which he has
postponed until Genl Grant arrives. But I have my

[5] Grant arrived in Chattanooga on the evening of October 23, 1863.

stove in the tent and a good floor, and am quite as comfortable barring the curtailed space as though I were in a house. Jesse is very well it is very pleasant to be so close to each other. Our old staff have all separated, and when we meet, we cannot help mourning for the absence of Genl Negley. I cannot help hoping though now that Genl Thomas will have him back here. Thomas holds him in high estimation. The cause of his leaving as developed is disgraceful to some general officers here who were jealous of him and not creditable at all to Genl R[osecrans] who was influenced by them. But I wont put it on paper, I will tell you when I see you. . . . as ever your true husband

Alfred

Head-quarters Department of the Cumberland
Office Commissary of Musters
Chattanooga Oct 28 1863
My Dearest Wife

. . . I personally am about in the same condition as last quoted, in comfortable quarters, and getting *wholesome* food to eat. But as a whole our army is just passing through an ordeal, that will soon decide its fate and I feel almost certain now that all is right. I have nothing else to write about so will have to make a military letter. I have made a rough sketch of our situation which I enclose. The outside line of [word omitted] is our line of battle now, the line through the town we are now building for permanent fortification. The rebels are immediately in front of our line, and amuse themselves by throwing shells from a battery on old Lookout, indicated by a cross, and they hardly reach us so we don't worry about them. They also have occupied the north bank of the river all the way down to

Stevenson thereby preventing us from using either the river or railroad, which runs on the south side to Bridgeport 10 miles from Stevenson. Consequently we had to wagon our supplies away round over Walder's ridge, the river road being commanded by them also. Well the rains have so damaged the roads, that hauling could not be done, so one of three things had to be done—open the river, retreat, or starve. First we sent the horses to the rear after about one-third of them died, oh it was dreadful to see them, poor creatures, then we went on half rations ourselves, that aint so bad, for there are very few men can eat a whole ration. In the mean time the plans were being laid for opening the river but this was known only to the leading few. We have been building pontoons for some time, which was supposed to be for another bridge in front of the town. But night before last two Brigades were quietly marched across the river and down to a point marked Brown's ferry at the foot of Strangers Ridge, 1000 of them were left behind and placed in the pontoons, they slipped down with the current past 4 miles of rebel pickets and landed opposite Brown's ferry, rushed up the hill, and overpowered the pickets, the pontoons then ferried over the others and in an hour from the first landing we had 5000 men with artillery on the hill, and before the rebs could bring a large force against them, they had entrenched themselves and reported themselves impregnable, and by 9 A.M. they had the pontoon bridge laid, and there they are yet—casualties 4 killed & 17 wounded. Our men did not fire a gun, but worked. It was as fine a thing as was ever done. Genl [William F.] Smith Chief Engineer planned it, and Genls [John S.] Tu[r]chin and [William B.] Hazen commanded the troops. So far so good. We had a lodgement on the rebel side, but still the rebels occupied

Raccoon Mountain, which you see almost fills the bend made by the river, and we wondered all day yesterday what would be the next thing done, but about 12 last night we were awakened by heavy artillery away off down the river, we never get up for artillery, so were about turning over to go to sleep, when the long rumbling sound of musketry was heard very soon hundreds were up and wondering where it was, it was certainly not on our line, but soon it leaked out. Hooker had crossed the river and Raccoon Mountain, away down lower than my map will show, and had marched up to the position marked on the map almost making a connection with our troops that had crossed at Brown's ferry, and would have done so soon, thereby bagging some thousand rebels on the promontory of Raccoon Mt,—but Longstreet thought he had gone far enough, and attacked him in force, the fight raged terribly for two hours, the result was Longstreet was repulsed at all points, but during the fight most of the rebs on Raccoon escaped. I have not heard the number of casualties, but it must be considerable the fighting was heavy your friend Genl [John W.] Geary's Div. did the heaviest of the fighting. This morning the two armies joined on the north side of the river, and we now have control of the river from Prince's ferry to Stevenson, and I don't think they can dislodge us, 24 hours more, and we will feel certain, and then oh what visions of good food again.[6] I would like to see bread and butter once again.

Now there's a military letter for you and as I have nothing else to say will close . . .

Alfred

[6] See Thomas B. Van Horne, *The Life of Major General George H. Thomas*, pp. 157-160, for an account of this action. Also Freeman Cleaves, *Rock of Chickamauga, The Life of General George H. Thomas*, Norman, 1948, p. 189.

Just after finishing the last sheet I was summoned to Genl Thomas' presence, he wanted information about the prospect of the Veteran Vol. Recruiting, and my aroused feelings caused by my recent writing made me almost eloquent on the subject, some of my suggestions will be adopted by him I think. If we could have some plan, some system adopted, by which these brave fellows who are now living on half rations and half clothes could go home for 30 days, we could reenlist the majority of them. I have given my whole mind to this subject, and as the staff officer at Headquarters in my department I am looked to for information, I feel as if I was of some use here, and that is a source of satisfaction to me though it gives me no honor before the world.

It seems as though I were visited with inspiration on this subject just at this time, for since I penned the last sentence I have been attending to business, and the case before me was a living witness of what I have been writing about. A fine looking gentlemanly educated young man named Chas. Stewart of Philadelphia, presented himself for muster in to the 15th Pa Cavalry (The Anderson Troop). He was in the battle of Stone River, got sick from exposure, and was discharged for disability—went home recovered his health, and now has come all the way down here to reenlist. After mustering him, I made some complimentary remarks upon his patriotism in coming back again after his severe experience. He replied almost sorrowfully I thought, "Well Captain I could not stay at home, I went into the war as a duty, and when I went back I found my friends so different from what they used to be that I was not happy. They had formed themselves into insurance associations, to insure one another against the draft by paying the exemption fee, and fathers and brothers who had sons or brothers in the army were trying to get them out again, it disgusted me so that I was in a continual wrangle, and when I got entirely well, my own arguments with others told me I ought to go back again, and I have come. I tell you, Captain, patriotism at the north is about finished, they only think of how much money they can make out of the war." From the sacrifices of such men will this country build its greatness upon, and when all is over, what will they be, almost paupers living in the presence of a moneyed aristocracy, built upon the profits made by filling the graves of hundreds of thousands of their fellow countrymen. This selfish unpatriotic feeling, is the real cause of Copperheadism men who are really for the Government (provided it don't take anything but money from them) and have supported it, when they fear that they even may be called upon to give themselves fly to *Peace* principles as a refuge and talk about this "useless war". I tell you Mary as sick as I am of war and bloodshed, as much oh how much, as I want to be home with my dear wife and children, I could not conscientiously deprive my country of my humble services while in the prime of life, nor could I bear to think of what my children would be if we were to permit this Hellbegotten conspiracy to destroy this country.

But my pen runs wild on this subject, and will close it, and will try not to touch upon it for the future, but if any of my friends want to know my sentiments you may read them what I have written.

About myself I am very happy where I am and would not want to go anywhere else unless it was to be with Genl Negley. . . . Genl Negley will ask for me himself, and if he don't get me, I must content myself with the assurance that the Government thinks I am more useful where I am. As I said before I have some reputation made here, and a large acquaintance which I think esteems me, and with that I must be satisfied as much as a soldier can be who has as much ambition as I have. As you suggest I would not be at all surprised if Genl Negley came back now that Genl Thomas is in command. If he had not left I know he never would have done so, but now that he has gone, there may be some difficulties in the way that cannot be overcome. As long as I stay in the Dept I have no fear of not being pleasantly situated, I may be changed about, but not to my discomfort. Genl Thomas treats me very kindly I think he fully understands me. You feared I was not well because I wrote so despondently, I have not been sick, am in most excellent health. If I am sick will tell you of it. I do not know when I can have the clothes sent, but you get them ready as soon as possible, and when I think it safe to send them will let you know. I want quite a lot of other things, and when I get paid will send the money for you to get them for me and send them altogether. . . .

> Your true husband,
> Alfred

Head-quarters Department of the Cumberland,
Office Commissary of Musters
Chattanooga Tenn Nov. 4, 1863
My Dearest Mary

. . . You ask me what I think of the war and whether we can end it before the time that part of our army goes out of existence next summer. This is a question that too many of our people at home are asking, depending on *us* to finish this war. Have they no responsibility resting upon them? Have they no patriotism? Are they not prepared to make some sacrifices? These are questions put in good faith I fear they have not. They are like the weak-hearted man that thinks he is benevolent, when he gives alms to a beggar to be rid of his presence, rather than go and help him out of degradation or crime. We are beginning to feel that our people at home do not yet understand their responsibility. They are more extravagant, more luxurious and I am afraid more dissolute to-day, than when their brothers, sons and husbands left them. They will give, give, give in money, but will they give themselves, no, they will not we have too much evidence of it in the recent draft, they are willing, very willing to pay $300.00 for exemption, and congratulate themselves that they are doing their duty and rail at the Copperheads for opposing the Government,—while they are giving this money, they are making double the amount through the very existence of this dreadful war the speculation produced by it gives them opportunities they never had before, on one side is the enhancement of the value of everything, causing an additional percentage of profit, on the other side they are relieved of competition by the absence of active energetic fellows, that are fighting for the existence of their country, or are lying in unknown graves. The extravagance among you is dreadful, we see it in the advertisements of the papers, we talk about it much, and the state of morals we are satisfied is worse than formerly. I cannot but think of the French revolution when I read the northern papers. . . . Just look at the difference to be sure coffee, sugar, tea, bread, fuel, clothing, all the necessaries of life are higher, than before the war, but so are wages, so are profits, and in greater proportion. How

is it with us. Our salaries are no higher, and yet we have
just as much and more, much more in many cases to
pay for our daily living. Our pay is just the same now,
as it was when gold was at par, now gold is 50 percent
premium, which is equivalent to reducing our pay one-
third. We would not complain of this if it was appreciated by our money-making friends at home but it is not,
they look upon us as well paid for our services taking a
commercial view of the whole matter. No my dear wife,
things must change. The rebellion will be put down.
This army will put it down *in time,* if not by next summer, then the next, if not then, another summer. I say
this army for more than half of our troops will become
veteran volunteers. They will never lay down their arms
till the country is eased. But if you will give us your
men, we will put down this monster so much the sooner.
If Congress will only repeal the exemption law, we will
get a new army and finish the war, if they do not, every
man drafted will pay his $300.00 and *we* will have to
fight it out and you may look for several years more of
war. I sometimes think it would be better for us if our
finances became bankrupt, for then the tie that binds
our men to money and pleasure would be broken, and
they would be compelled to go to war to reestablish
themselves. A conscience scared critic might say upon
reading my remarks, Oh it is all very well for him to
talk he is an officer, if I could go as an officer I would
go too. Let me say to him, *more than two-thirds* of the
officers of the army at present, went into this war as
privates like myself. And if we after having borne the
heat and burthen of the day, have risen a little from the
heaviest labor, it is no more than fair that they who
have been resting in the shade, should now perform
some work. I could say much more on this subject if I

had time, but I have filled up my sheet and will have to start another to finish my letter on. But be a soldier's wife, and tell the men their duties, at the same time as a soldier's wife let the women of your acquaintance understand that they can do much harm, by encouraging the present existing extravagance.

A. L. H.

Head-quarters Department of the Cumberland
Office Commissary of Musters
Chattanooga Nov 18 1863
My Dearest Mary
. . . As I told you in my note of Monday (enclosing the check for $200.00) I was sick, I am still under the weather suffering now from the effects of a dose of salts! but no doubt will be all right in a day or two. You write as feeling more cheerful about us and think Chattanooga safe. You are perfectly right, we have no fear now of being cut off from our supplies. Our force is strong, communications well guarded, supplies coming in regularly, and nothing but a pitched battle in which we should be beaten can drive us off, which latter I don't think would be the case, I feel very certain it would not. But as to our going any further that is another matter. Our animals are all dead or used up, and another supply must be had before we leave the railroad and river. Another stoppage has been put upon my personal movements, and unintentionally so by a friend. At Genl Negley's request, when he left I wrote to a mutual friend supposed to have influence at Washington to assist him in getting me detailed, in case the General did not get to Washington. Well this friend in his goodness of heart, and innocence of red tape, wrote to one of the Ass Adt Generals, urging my detail, he re-

ferred it through the proper channel to my immediate
commander, which of course he would do. Genl Thomas
sent it back with this endorsement "Respectfully returned, Capt Hough is on duty at these Headquarters
as A C M and is too valuable an officer to be spared as
an A. D. C." Of course I feel complimented at the
endorsement, but "I don't see" the benefit of it. In the
meantime Genl Negley asks verbally and gets the permission, but now Genl Thomas' protest is on record,
and I don't think Genl Negley would like to push it, I
would not much certainly. I wrote to the General at
Nashville about it, and he can take what course he
chooses. *I* would not go against Pop Thomas' wishes
for a million. I don't know what command Genl Negley
will have; he is in Nashville now and has been there for
ten days. I was much concerned at your remarks about
your required economy, but have been expecting it for
some time, have been intending to write to you about it
but have put the evil day off and off. Now my dearest
you must look the matter square in the face, and make
your plans to meet the circumstances. As I wrote you
some time ago the people at home who are making
money do not really understand the sacrifices we are
making. My sense of duty and honor would not permit
me to leave the service while this rebellion existed. Yet
I know if I were to leave it now my experience and
knowledge of the present times would enable me to make
money out of the war as our friends at home are doing.
Yet while I am here I cannot only not make any money
but must live on smaller means than before the war
commenced. I live with the most rigid economy, depriv-
ing myself of everything but the necessaries of life, even
clothing which I ought to have I cannot afford to buy,
with the exception of the dress coat, I wear soldier's

clothes, and that coat I husband with all care, (this is the case with all officers who have not other means than their salaries that have families). And yet withal I send every cent I have over and above my expenses to my family. And that you know is no more than you used to get when prices were very different. Now my dearest you are a soldier's wife, and must help bear his burthens, trusting that the time will come when you can have your reward. To sum up the whole matter my dear, you know what it formerly cost us to live, and the prices we paid. And now at the present prices it is equivalent to living on $1,000 per annum, and the family divided. And it may be worse yet my dearest, so hard as it is, it is my duty to ask you to suit yourself to the circumstances, as I know you have the heart to do if necessary. While the children are young we can make this sacrifice, and I trust before their expenses increase circumstances will be changed. This is all I have to say, and it is very hard for me to say it. . . . as ever yours

Alfred

Nashville Dec 30/63 [7]

My Dearest Mary

Here I have been two days and likely to remain several days more. Upon getting here I found Capt Young absent at Washington, and information for me that

[7] During the period from November 18 to December 30 Hough was home on sick leave. Since there were no letters during this period, the story can be picked up in his manuscript autobiography.

"The surgeon said a change of climate was absolutely necessary, and that I had better go home, especially as the Army was about to move on the enemy and Chattanooga would probably be filled with wounded men. I was granted a leave on his certificate and with great difficulty I rode to the river and got on a boat at Kellys ferry, being too sick to be even interested in the advance of the troops which was then going on, the beginning of the fight at Lookout Mountain, the beginning of

makes it important that I should see him before I go
to the front. So I reported by telegraph to Chattanooga
and am on duty here till his return. I sincerely hope it
wont be many days for of all the disgusting places I
find this is the worst I ever experienced. It is neither
one thing or the other. It has all the disagreeables of
the army without its pleasures, and you are in the very
worst of the experiences of civil life, all the trash that
follows an army you find here, besides that I paid $3.00
per day board, and last night my room was entered and
I was robbed fortunately I had my pocket book and
watch under my pillow, but my clothes were rifled, losing about $2.00 in change. . . . I have now changed
my quarters and am sleeping at Genl Rousseau's Head-
quarters (on the floor) and eating at a restaurant, so
it wont be quite as expensive for me. I have not a great
deal to do in the way of business, but meet so many of
my old friends here, that I spend the time very pleasantly, when I can forget the evils of the place.[8]

---

the great contest then coming on, was in full view as I rode wearily
along through Lookout Valley to the ferry.

"Whether it was the change of air, or the prospect of seeing my
beloved family, or both combined, I do not know, but every days travel
improved me and when I reached Philadelphia I was much better and
pronounced by the surgeon convalescent. A happy reunion, only too
short and I was soon well enough to retrace my steps, and on the 28th
of December I was again in Nashville en route to Chattanooga, where
I found orders for me to remain till the Chief Commissary returned
from Washington where he had gone on important business connected
with the mustering of Veteran Volunteers."

[8] Hough's Autobiography furnishes a more complete picture of the
changes in Nashville. By the time he made his later judgments he was
more aware of the transition wrought by war and less concerned about
losing $2.00 out of his pants pocket.

"In 1862 it [Nashville] was a beautiful city, handsome stores, pretty
home-like dwellings, and clean streets in the city, and fine suburban
residences with an abundance of shade around it. The years of war,
with it for a depot, and for three months during Buell's retreat to
Kentucky besieged, had changed it. The streets were simply mud pits
when it rained, and dust heaps when it did not; the houses had lost
their freshness of look; wooden shanties were stuck in many of the

I have only borrowed a place at a desk, and here comes its owner, will continue this on a future occasion. Will only say though that I *positively* go to Chattanooga to stay. With all love Good bye

Alfred

Head-quarters Department of the Cumberland,
Office Commissary of Musters
Jan 9th 1864

My Dearest Mary:

It is very well that I directed you to send your letters here for the future, for lo! and behold! as poor dear mother used to say, here I am to remain, at least this is my station. I have been regularly appointed by a Dept order Inspector of the Mustering Dept, with my office with Capt Young at Nashville Chief Mustering officer under whose instructions I act and to whom I report. My duties will carry me over the whole department, and I am only waiting for the cold snap to get over before I make a start for Chattanooga and Knoxville. I think I shall like the position, it will be interesting at least, though travelling during the winter will be rather rough work I think my first trip will occupy about a month, and when I come back I will move up bag and baggage. At present I am faring rather hard I cannot afford to board at a hotel & cannot get private boarding, so am sleeping in the office and live at restaurants. My cot and blankets being at Chattanooga, I am rather

yards of the fine residences, and the whole city was filled with that most unwholesome class, 'Camp followers.' Around the city fences and trees were all gone, bare houses stood in the midst of desolation, and I could ride in any direction without regard to roads or fences. The place was full of people but very little was seen of the old inhabitants, most of them were Rebel sympathizers and secluded themselves; the troops of the garrison were generally in their quarters and consquently most of the people seen were camp followers, and the lower class of inhabitants, not at all desirable companions."

short of bed clothing for this cold weather I have bought some blankets but will have to get some more if I expect to keep warm. It is wonderful how long this cold weather continues. It is quite as severe a winter as I have experienced for some years, the poor people in the country are suffering dreadfully, our soldiers with few exceptions are in winter quarters and are comfortable. Our department is very busy now in mustering in vet volunteers, if Congress will renew the bounty we will get almost all of them. How happy they do look on their way home I expect they will cut up some shindys when they get there, but you must bear with them, for they are brave fellows and have only one short month of recreation before returning here to fight more battles and leave some of their number to add to the thousands of graves that now mark the scenes of their former work. The 7th Pa. Cavalry one of the best regiments in the service is being mustered into the vet service to-day at our office, one of the companies is from Lock Haven, and upon looking at the names I found I knew many of their families, and when I talked to them of their friends how happy they looked, some of them I found remembered me, they are a splendid looking set of young men. This mustering of veterans is delightful, I feel like loving every one of them.

    . . . as ever, your true and loving husband
                                    Alfred

    Head-quarters Department of the Cumberland
    Office Commissary of Musters
    Chattanooga Jan 31/64
My Own Dear Wife
    I find everything here much changed, the troops have all taken up new positions the cold weather has caused

all the timber for miles around to be cleared for fuel, earth works cover every hill, and worst of all graveyards cover several places that were green fields when I saw them last. When I look around 'tis hard to realize that this is the same place that we entered on the 31st of Sept only four months since. A thriving pretty town, with fine residences surrounded with ornamental grounds with the adjacent country relieved by alternate enclosed fields and beautiful woods, in four short months to be changed to a desert waste, not a tree or fence for miles every house a barrack or hospital, and nothing growing but graveyards, but such is war. Oh how horrible it is, may this terrible one soon end. I find everything as regards the welfare of the troops, in much better condition than when I left. The railroad is open through to here, the men are clothed, in comfortable cabins and have full rations, their health is fair much better than last winter, and all in good spirits. The veterans are leaving all the time, and new recruits are coming in. When the veterans return what a fine army we will have. Old Lookout no more frowns on us with an enemy's guns, but our own stars and stripes float there in full view. Before I leave I intend going up there for a look at the country and anticipate a rich treat.

As to future operations I can ascertain nothing, I do not think though that anything will be done before spring excepting cavalry operations I think our cavalry will operate pretty freely from this time out.

From the number of deserters and refugees that are coming in I am satisfied the rebellion is not flourishing since the battle of Chickamauga 9000 deserters were recorded here and at Knoxville, that is an army of itself. I think I shall be here about a week, and then

return to Nashville stopping by the way. I may go to
Knoxville, but think not. I am here interrupted and
will not have time to write more before the mail
closes. . . .

                                        Alfred

                              Chattanooga Feb 6th 1864
My Dearest Mary
    . . . Here I am on the old ground and very busy.
I have not been relieved from my old position and my
station is still at Nashville, but have been ordered to
assume additional duties temporarily. Capt [Gideon
C.] Moody has gone home on leave with the intention
of resigning when he gets there if he can. I am acting
as C M for the Corps in his place until his return, and
have my old duties at Headquarters of Genl Thomas
besides. I shall be here for 20 days certain and perhaps
permanently so you may see I am *very* busy. I find
things very much changed since I left, very few troops
in the town, all of them out at different points some 10
or 12 miles distant. The ranks have been much advanced, and the place could be defended by a small
force. Supplies are abundant and this is an important
depot. The late movement in front, was only a demonstration to occupy Johns[t]on to keep him from moving on Sherman, which was effectually done. We have
had no war news from other armies for some time
owing to the lines being down, and are anxious to hear
from Sherman and others, as we suppose of course that
other armies are busy like ourselves. We are occupying
a pretty large force in front of us reaching from Virginia to Miss. Our army has seen its weakest point, the
veterans have not all gone yet, but more are coming
back now, than are going home, in a month we will be

very strong. I was out to see the Colored Regiment on
dress parade to-day, and was much pleased, and am
now really looking anxiously for the time for my taking
command of my own. If it was not for the dead mules
lying around town, I could enjoy riding around, for it
is really beautiful here naturally. The new cemetery is
coming on, the bodies are almost all in it, a heavy
stone wall is being built around it, and what I have
never seen here before is, some of the graves are being
decorated by loving friends. Speaking of the cemetery
reminds me of a scene I witnessed yesterday. I went to
see a friend who was wounded badly in the late movement, Col. Michelotzi [9] he is a German long in this
country, has been wounded four times but this one is a
very serious one, and he was reported killed; his wife
is here with him, a sharp determined Yankee woman.
She was speaking of her troubles on her way here, saying she was met by the remark every where that there
was no use of her going that the Col was dead, and his
body could be sent on. When she got this far the Col.
raised his head, and spoke with great firmness, "I have
put my veto on that, if I die my body does not go from
here, but must lie with my men on yonder hill"; how
it thrilled me, too hard for such men to die young. . . .
Our living is fair, not good, but better than when I was
here last, and we have plenty of it. I am satisfied there
will be a grand movement from here some time this
spring, but when I cannot say; heavy trains and extras
for draft and artillery are now marching down from
Nashville. Well I see I am getting into my old way
talking about war, but there really is nothing else to
talk about. . . .

Alfred

[9] Colonel Geza Mihalotzy, Third Brigade, Fourteenth Army Corps.

Head-quarters Department of the Cumberland
Office of Commissary of Musters
Chattanooga March 13th 1864
My Dearest Mary:

. . . My Dear Mary your necessary economy is very trying to me, I know it must be so although you said nothing about it, and it will yet be worse. I have hard work to live here on what I allow for myself, and we can only hope that a more stable state of affairs will soon prevail. Indeed we may be thankful we are as well off as we are. I feel so when I look around and see the thousands of poor refugees leaving their homes, the land they have owned and lived upon for years, and travelling hundreds of miles with their young children and living upon the cold charity of the government. This is a terrible ordeal we are going through, but out of this darkness we will appear brighter and better, so I believe, and every day I have a more religious feeling, that this war is a crusade for the good of mankind. If you could only see what we are doing for the blacks, you would be astonished. The regiment stationed here, only four months organized, have now over one-third that can read, learned since they left the plantations. This indicates what will be done; so my dearest we must bear our share of the burthen, but for all that I feel deeply most deeply your privations, and no sacrifice will be too great for me to enable you to be comfortable. At the same time I do not wish you to think that money has influenced me in being willing to change my position. It may have had some effect, for I feel my poverty greatly, but the two most controlling influences are first, duty and an inclination to exhibit personally my belief in what I have advocated so strongly against prejudice, and secondly, ambition, and future preferment. My present duties are very pleasant to me and useful to the country, but are not of such a nature as to push me forward in the future.

In regard to the danger, there is no more than being with white troops, and if I do not get this regiment I fully expect to be with my own command as soon as the work of mustering is over, and I see no difference between fighting with whites, or fighting with black troops. So don't worry my dearest wife and continue the trust in Providence you always have had. As yet I know nothing of the matter. I am promised the Regiment if I will accept it which I have agreed to do if I can get leave of absence to accept, the leave has been asked for and we are waiting for an answer, the chances are rather against its being granted, but I *will not* resign my present position to accept the other.[10] So there is a plain history of how I stand and how I have been guided, but in all likelihood I shall be in the line again by the time the camp again opens either in one way or the other, because I think I can be more useful there after a while but it may be different if so circumstances will govern me. You speak of my health, I am very well, and fortunately very busy, for if it were not for business time would hang heavy on my hands, it is very dull here now, the troops are all some miles out to the

10 "Colored troops were being raised, and the Commissioner for their organization offered me a colonelcy. I agreed to accept, provided I could get permission from the War Dept. to do so without affecting my position in the Regular Army. The Commissioner applied for me and he was refused on the ground that I could not be spared from my then duties. This failure again proved fortunate for me, as most of the colored troops raised in Nashville did nothing but laboring duty there and I would not have had an opportunity of doing anything with them in the field." Alfred Lacey Hough, Manuscript Autobiography.

front, only a garrison here, and headquarters. And oh how desolate it looks not a tree for miles and nothing to be seen but the remains of camps, which look and smell terribly. The natural beauties of the place are great, but we have temporarily destroyed them, the distant view though relieves the eye and at any time you can feast upon mountain scenery. The sunset view here as Phoebus sinks below the crest of the hills is grand, and I never tire of looking at it.

My friend the Colonel who I told you about is dead and today we buried him—"with his boys on yonder hill". We all feel deeply his loss, he was a true man and a soldier, peace to his ashes. Oh dear I wish I could see you and the little ones. Give them kisses for me . . . and accept all love from your true husband,

Alfred

Chattanooga Monday morning March 21, 1864
My Dearest Mary:

. . . My clerk said to me yesterday while I was reading your letter, "Captain, it always does me good to hand you a letter from your wife". "Why", replied I? "Because you always look so happy when you get it, and then while you are reading it, you always laugh so quietly, that I think of Mrs. Hough and wonder if she is not always full of fun". Now there's a criticism upon you, it is Charlie's sayings that always convulse me with laughter. You appear to emulate Mark Tapley and are jolly under adverse circumstances. I always like to see you taking the bright side of life, and enjoy what pleasures are around you. . . . As ever your true husband

Alfred

HEAD-QUARTERS
FOURTEENTH ARMY CORPS,
Office Commissary of Musters
Chattanooga, March 23, 1864

My Dearest Mary

. . . I have not heard a word about my black Regiment lately and I suppose it has fallen through. I don't believe now that I could be relieved from mustering. Capt Moody was resigned and only Capt Young and myself are left who thoroughly understand the business. Capt Y is sick at present, and I am really managing the whole department, quite a huge affair. We have 19 officers in the Dept, and besides my share of mustering you would be astonished at the number of papers referred to me for information.[11] And so many officers come personally for information that I have been compelled to fix office hours that I can have a time for business with papers when I see no one. This rush of business has gratified me in one respect. I have been astonished at how much business I can do when it is forced upon me. I find the more that is put upon me, the more quickly my mind adapts itself to the work, my ideas come quick, and I decide at once. I do not get overwhelmed with business, I master it, and have mastered more lately than I supposed I could do. I really believe I ought to have been a professional man, I am afraid I am spoilt for teaching, if there is anything I have a contempt for now it is a teacher, this is confidential I know it is wrong, but I have the feeling, and it is

11 An official report made by Captain John H. Young on March 5, 1864, indicates why Captain Hough was so busy. "Twenty-six thousand five hundred veterans enlisted up to 1st instant. Fifteen hundred additional reported unofficially. Am confident will reach 30,000." Captain General, March 5, 1864, *O. R.* Series I, Vol. XXXII, Part III, Correspondence, 25.

honest. So I am afraid it will be my lot to be poor and proud for the rest of my life.

. . . your true and loving husband

Alfred

HEAD-QUARTERS DEPARTMENT
OF THE CUMBERLAND
Office Commissary of Musters
Nashville, Monday April 4th 1864

My Dearest Wife:

. . . Tuesday. I feel so much annoyed this morning that I cannot avoid relieving myself by telling you of my troubles although I did not intend to till I knew how matters would terminate. You have often heard me speak and write of Capt Young the Chief Mustering officer of the Dept. For nearly a year now I have been under him, and among some twenty officers I have become next in position to him and he has depended on me to a great extent. I have often noticed what an extraordinary man he was for business, a mind of more than ordinary power, of habits the most exemplary in the matter of drinking never touching a drop. What was my astonishment some two months since to see him come into the office intoxicated, he remained so for days constantly drinking, and his old friends told me, he was subject to such attacks about once a year, that we ought to overlook it and in fact protect him. He went on till he got sick and then repentant. I then talked with him and he was very thankful for my forbearance, and promised not to touch another drop, &c., &c. In the meantime I have been attending to all the business which accounts for my being so busy lately. I supposed all would be right. But when I came up here, I found him still drinking, and in such a state he could give me no coherent instructions, but started immediately for Chattanooga, previously placing an officer in arrest illegally. The officer was released by order of Genl Thomas, hence the trouble I spoke of, I have not heard a word of him since. And whether he is in trouble at the front, or whether he has sobered up and explained matters satisfactorily I cannot tell. But in the meantime it leaves me very much unsettled. I am not stationed here *by order* as I expected to be and to remain under him as I have been, I cannot conscientiously, as I told him when I talked to him that I would not if he kept on drinking. He is shrewd enough to conceal his failing from the General, and of course I would not expose him, as the business is all attended to. I am very much annoyed, and fully expect I shall be compelled by my own self to ask to be sent to my Regiment.—Now I have told you all and I feel relieved I have concealed this trouble from you hoping it would pass away. What a terrible thing it is, to see a man of his calibre and good heart so degraded by a miserable vice. Good-bye for to-day.

Wednesday: I feel in better spirits this morning not that I have any news from Young, only that with my usual philosophy I have accepted the issue, and am simply waiting for the denouement, prepared for going to my Regiment or whatever else may occur. I am boarding now at a real nice place, a lady keeps it and keeps it well, good table and pleasant officers at table, price $7.00 per week. My servant boards at a colored boarding house at $2.50. This is about as cheap as I can live anywhere in the field now.

. . . Remember me to all, and believe me as ever your true husband

Alfred

HEAD-QUARTERS
DISTRICT OF NASHVILLE,
Office Commissary of Musters,
Nashville, Tenn., April 27th, 1864

My Dearest Mary:

. . . We are about having stirring times everything
is being rushed to the front, horses will be passed to-
day on, Northern cities for cavalry and all troops in
the Western states, whether ready or not are ordered
here as a reserve and to be instructed, all old troops
are ordered to the front. We shall have an immense
camp here and plenty to do. As you say I have no doubt
Capt Y will be relieved, but I have no idea I will get the
place, somebody of more rank will get it, besides I
fully expect now to take the Colored Regiment. I shall
not ask to be sent to my own Regiment under any circumstances, but it is not at all impossible I shall be
ordered there as they are sending almost all detached
officers to their Regiments, but I don't see how I can
be spared now for a while anyhow, but they may not
know that at Washington. . . . God be with us now
for a few short weeks will decide whether we have
speedy peace or a long internecine war. We are not as
well prepared as we ought to have been we have plenty
of *men,* but they have been so slow in sending them forward that the new ones are a mere mob as yet, and
those we have at least 10000 dismounted cavalry here
and in the states, we are going to put them in the rear
as a reserve dismounted. Good bye God bless you. . . .

                                                        Alfred

HEAD-QUARTERS
DISTRICT OF NASHVILLE,
Nashville, Tenn., May 1st 1864

My Dearest Mary:

. . . By the time this reaches you I am pretty certain we will have either a fight, or a retreat of the enemy, I think the former. From the way we have been moving troops, I am satisfied this week will bring matters to a head. While the whole country is looking to the Army of the Potomac, they will be surprised to hear of active operations here before they move. The enemy also will be astonished I think, we are stronger than is supposed. . . .

I will be relieved of Adjutant General's duties tonight and shall not be quite so busy. I shall know in a day or two about my Colored Regiment. Capt Massey [Mussey] has telegraphed to Washington for my services for military reasons. Capt Y[oung] is behaving badly still and I am attending to his business. If the War Dept knew of his condition he could not stand a day, but the business is attended to and they know nothing of it. They must wonder though at my acting for so long a time and the Captain here all the time. So goes the world.

I have performed a deal of work the last week and have no little satisfaction in knowing that I have done all put before me and a good deal of a kind I never did before. The General would tell me to write letters to such and such Commanders, merely mentioning the subject, and it has been during a specially busy time. We have placed troops along the whole line of road from here to Chattanooga, and all the old ones have been

pushed forward to the front. . . . as ever your true
husband

Alfred

HEAD-QUARTERS
DISTRICT NASHVILLE,
Office Commissary Musters,
Nashville, Tenn., May 5th, 1864

My Dearest Mary

. . . We have been pushing everything to the front
for the last week leaving the line of communication
very bare of troops. Our force in the front is strong,
and if successful it will make no difference, but if we are
unsuccessful look out for a raid on the line and perhaps
on Nashville. This is an immense storehouse. The larg-
est military depot in the world at this moment I expect. Every storehouse is full and acres of stuff are
piled up around the town. We must hold Nashville at
all hazards, all Government employees are enrolled
and armed for defence if necessary, we could raise quite
an army besides the Garrison which is quite small and
they would fight well behind fortifications. At this
moment I expect they are fighting at the front. The
movement commenced yesterday, and a fight must soon
follow, I have every confidence in our success although
[J. E.] Johns[t]on has a pretty good army in front of
us and the country is easily defended. But the morale
of our army is grand, it exceeds anything we have had
before, health good, spirits good, well clothed plenty to
eat, &c., &c. I wish I could feel as confident of the
Potomac Army, but I *may* be mistaken in both of them.
It is strange but I feel an itching to be at the front, but
I have no business there so wont go. I fear I shall

continue to muster till the war ends. I have just received my quietus about the Colored Regiment. The War Department have answered saying I cannot have leave to accept it, that ends the matter much to my disgust and I may say anger. There is a futility about my advancement. Always recommended for merit and always refused because it is not expedient this time I have no doubt it is because I cannot be spared as a mustering officer. And because I am a good mustering officer which very few are I must be kept a captain, while plenty of numbskulls, not half my equals in capacity are made Field officers of Volunteers and Colored troops Oh! the injustice of such things. Well I have my consolation I am doing my duty and am doing it so well they want to keep me where I am, but oh, it is hard to be kept down, and kept poor too. I never was so poverty stricken in my life I can barely live decently. I spend *nothing* after living except for books, and my enjoyment of life consists of performing my duties, riding before breakfast and before supper, reading in the evening and thinking of you all the time. If I could feel that I was to stay here I should most certainly have you here, but I know that cannot be. I am doing all Capt Young's business and either I shall have to go to the front and take his place, or quit altogether, one or the other must be done soon. If the War Dept knew of his condition they would relieve him at once, but they don't know of it, it is outrageous. But as officers in authority here know of it I shall remain silent and work, such is my lot. . . . God bless you all as ever your true husband

Alfred

HEAD-QUARTERS
DISTRICT NASHVILLE,
Office Commissary Musters,
Nashville, Tenn., May 8th, 1864

My Dearest Mary:

. . . Everything is quiet here, the weather is warm
and everything is green. We are waiting anxiously to
hear the result of the clash in front, have not heard for
two days but have no doubt they are fighting. We have
the first news from the Potomac but it is very indefinite.
It looks well as far as it goes. Oh what a critical period
in the history of this country. But I feel confident of
success, never have felt so much so before. If our Army
is successful in front of Chattanooga they will make
sad work of Georgia. The massacre at Fort Pillow will
be avenged most terribly.[12] There will be but little left
on the route of our army. But if we should not be successful we will have all the work to do we shall want.
We are drilling our raw troops very industriously for
the protection of Nashville—destroy this place and our
army would have to fall back or starve.

In the mean time I am here in Nashville doing anything but "war" it seems to me, sitting in an office with
clerks for all the world like a counting house; indeed
Mary I don't feel right about it but I must obey. I kind
of feel though as if I should be ordered to the front
pretty soon, and be with the army if they advance.

. . . Nashville looks more pleasant in its coat of
green, and I really do enjoy my morning rides, after
getting out of town I can scamper for miles across the
country no fences to stop you, over green fields, across

[12] On April 12, 1864, Confederate General N. B. Forrest attacked
Fort Pillow, Tennessee, and allegedly massacred several hundred
Negro troops instead of taking them prisoner.

running brooks through groves of immense trees Oh! its fine. And I wish for you often! Well Good bye I must close. . . .

Alfred

HEAD-QUARTERS
DISTRICT NASHVILLE,
Office Commissary Musters,
Nashville, Tenn., May 18, 1864

My Dearest Mary

I have yours of 9th and 12th we are coming nearer to time again I rejoice with you at the success of our armies but do not enter as deeply as you into the sanguine belief of the enemies overthrow, we may yet lose this camp again, but I trust not. Grant has done all and more than I thought he would, and the chances are that he will accomplish the work, delay now is all in our favor. He has solved the problem of the enemies strength and position, and can bring up his reserves and open his war communications for the next attack. If he does not now attack and defeat him, I fully believe when Grant again moves it will be to the overthrow of our arch enemy, I have great faith in Butler's accomplishing something, he has two of the best men with him we have, Gilmore [13] and [Major General] Wm. F. Smith. I am a little disappointed at the results in front of it. Sherman has defeated Johns[t]on and is pursuing him but I expected him to capture him entire, I am afraid he will get off to Richmond, but we must hope and pray for success. To come down to personal matters I am not a little amused at your remarks about the Colored Regiment. You did "not object", but you "hope there will be no danger". I have no doubt you

[13] Major General Quincy Adams Gillmore.

were sincerely thankful when you got my letter stating
I had been refused permission. . . . as ever your true
husband

Alfred

. . . I send you Genl Negley's case,[14] the remarks are
just, and the finding is as I told you it would be.

HEAD-QUARTERS
DISTRICT NASHVILLE,
Office Commissary Musters,
Nashville, Tenn., June 5th, 1864

My Dearest Mary

. . . my constant and longing hope is that the war
will end, and I be so placed that I can have you with me
and that within a year at least. And this you may reasonably expect that if I am living when this war ends,
if I cannot have you with me, I shall leave the army if I
have to be a clerk or worse for the rest of my life, for
the world to me is nothing without you. And that is
what has provoked me so about my uncertainty here all
this time. If I had known I was to stay here I could
have had you with me, to be sure we would have had
to live very poorly huddled in one room, and expensive
at that, but how much better than being separated.
There is a terrible distress among officers' families
now, many who have always lived well on their pay,
have now had to let their families be supported by their
relations with gold at 190 it makes living about double
what it previously was, but I hope it is almost over, I
don't think you are right about Indianapolis though my

14 Hough had been sent to Louisville, Kentucky, as a witness before
the Court of Inquiry which was investigating the conduct of Generals
Crittenden, McCook and Negley at the Battle of Chickamauga. The
officers were cleared of any blame.

dear just calculate a little my dear. You *could not possibly* keep a house now on $720 a year, it is only equal to about $400 three years since, and how could you rent a house however small, and feed and clothe yourself and children on that. It is humiliating I know but we must bear it hoping for the future it is in a good cause. I could earn double what I am getting almost anywhere if I were out of the army, but I could not do it my duty is here, so help me bear it dearest our children will be repaid for it. I am just as uncertain as ever about my movements Capt Young is just as bad or worse than ever, and the only reason why he retains his position is that Genl Thomas being in the front knows nothing of it, and it is no time to inform him, I have been asked to bring charges against him so as to put him in arrest, but I wont do it, the business goes on all right, and when this campaign is ended something will be done. We are all very anxious about our army; they have been fighting every day for two weeks, gradually driving the rebels back, and although we are before Atlanta now like it is on the Potomac the decisive battle has not been fought. If we are victorious all will be bright here, but if we should lose it would be terrible. Grant is only about 25 miles now from his base of operations, Sherman is nearly 300, we are expecting every day to have a terrible raid on us here, but the crisis must soon come. You don't seem, to judge from the papers, to think much of our war out here, but there has been constant and terrible fighting, a loss of at least 2000 killed and wounded on each side, and *very few* prisoners, such fighting as is being now done both east and west cannot last much longer, the war must soon end. . . .

Alfred

Chattanooga June 13th 1864

My Dearest Mary

I arrived here safe and well this morning but very tired and sleepy only getting a few cat naps while sitting straight up on a hard board seat all night. I am going no farther but shall start back tomorrow stopping at numerous places, expecting to get back in about a week. . . .

Chattanooga looks much as usual but there are more store houses and more fortifications no news from the front more than you get from the papers I must notice though one great change brought before me on my journey down. If you will recollect a letter from me about one year ago describing the desolation around Murfreesboro, and the remark of a negro that he only wanted to raise corn enough to eat, and if we did not have a fight there he would be all right. Now one short year what a change The whole surrounding country including the very battlefield of Stone River excepting the graveyards, and forests is one vast cotton field, planted and owned or rented by Northern men, and worked by hired negroes. Who will say we are not progressing another year and most likely we can say the same of the country around Atlanta.

I made another effort while here to get out of the unpleasant position I am in but have failed. Genl Milne the Post Commander of Nashville is extremely anxious to have me inspector of the Post and offered it to me in a very complimentary letter, but I find I cannot get relieved from mustering under any circumstances, but I am promised faithfully that matters will be represented to Genl Thomas in regard to the Capt, [Young] which will make me all right after a while so I must wait and hope. All love to the children and the whole for yourself, from your true husband

Alfred

Columbia Tenn June 18th 1864

My Dearest Mary

I have just arrived here (45 miles from Nashville) after travelling all night from Huntsville and find the following despatch for me dated Hd Qm Dept of Cumb at Big Shanty Ga. June 17th "The Genl Comdg directs that you report to these Hd quarters without delay as Com of Musters. By Command of Maj Genl Thomas. Henry Stone A A G". The return train goes in a few hours and I must go with it. I will write to you from Chattanooga being too tired and sleepy to write now, must take a nap before I start. I don't suppose I shall remain at the front but a few days but if this matter is consummated I have no doubt my Hd quarters will be at Chattanooga but I will tell you all as soon as I can With all love I am your true and loving husband

Alfred

. . . Address as usual to Nashville for the present.

Chattanooga June 21/64

Dearest Mary

I am here so far on my way and am now more in the dark than ever. I find an order here not changing my position, but ordering me to report without delay to Headquarters in the field of duty. So I am still C M for Dist of Tenn. but detailed for special duty 300 miles from my Post. I have nothing with me but what I have on my back, no horse no servant no nothing, and my office in Nashville is running without me. It is a curious state of affairs and the only supposition I can put upon it, and I have some reason for thinking so,—is that they have got stuck in their business at the front as to who are entitled to be mustered and who not and have sent for me to straighten out matters. I have not heard a word from Capt Young, nor have any messages gone to him from the front, and he is still the chief in his office in Nashville. The whole thing is very mysterious, and I obey orders without asking questions, and in the next train I am off for Big Shanty. Thank God I am very well, and only too happy to think I am thought of sufficient use for the General Commdg to send for me when all of the officers in the Dept but three were nearer, and most of them immediately around him. Write as usual to Nashville until further notice, and you must not expect to hear from me again for a long time. If you hear nothing you may know I am well as I shall be *acting* on Genl Thomas' staff, and will be more prominent for public notice than in most any other position. You must forgive me dearest for not writing such letters as I would like to but I am so full of business, and my mind is on such a strain, that you must wait till I am settled.[15] I have had no regular sleep for some time, but shall take a good nap before starting

---

[15] "My duties as Inspector of Musters while not giving me much duty on the firing line, and in no way distinguished, were arduous. The troops were so much on the move and so little time given for mustering work, with new Commissions constantly coming from the Governors of States, that I had to oversee the work of my subordinates and push it. With all the industry I could enforce, many Officers went into action with Commissions for higher grades in their pockets, and were killed or fatally wounded and never mustered, and without being mustered their Commissions were not complete. This conflict, or apparent conflict between General and State Government is a great evil in the organization of a volunteer army." Alfred Lacey Hough, Manuscript Autobiography.

to-day. I hope to be at the front tomorrow. So good-
bye my dearest. . . .

Alfred

HEAD-QUARTERS DEPARTMENT
OF THE CUMBERLAND,
Camp 4 miles from Marietta
June 24th 1864

My Dearest Mary

Again in the field having run the gauntlet of Guerillas to this point. I was on the first train over a bridge
just rebuilt, and the next train after has not yet got in,
another bridge behind us having been destroyed immediately after we passed. Our train was loaded with
amunition [*sic*], and we were fortunate in getting
through. The Guerillas are getting troublesome, but
are not strong enough to attack the trains they only
make a dash and destroy the road causing delay; we
soon rebuild them and a stronger guard is now being
put on which we hope will prevent further trouble. I
find things in good condition. Our troops are fighting
every day gradually pushing the enemy before them.
The rebels have fallen into a strong position strongly
entrenched, which we are now attacking as I write the
roar of battle wages, but our Headquarters are out of
range. The troops are in good condition, plenty to eat,
but the work is very hard—fighting and digging. Our
losses though are not so heavy as I supposed. We will
take Atlanta but it will be some time yet and through
some hard fighting. But about myself, I find I am ordered here for immediate duty to straighten up matters
neglected by Capt Young, and an application has gone
to Washington for my appointment as Chief Com of

Musters for the Dept to relieve Capt Young; until an answer comes I am only temporarily here. I have no doubt it will be granted, and most likely after going to the rear to arrange matters I shall return here to stay, but until it is decided I can only speculate. I must admit though I feel much gratified at the compliment of being sent for to fill this position. I shall be in a strait though for the present having no change of clothing or anything else—fortunately I find a cot of an absent officer which I am using. I am very well though my ride from Chattanooga of two days on top of a car was very tiresome ending with a walk of six miles through the sun carrying my bundle; but I feel like an old campaigner already and fall into the routine as natural as life. I am sorry about one thing, I cannot send you any money from here, if I get back to Chattanooga I can send you some. . . . Now dearest I believe I have told you all, and as I am writing under very great difficulties surrounded by fellow staff officers who are constantly bothering me with questions, and tendering messages to you also timing me as they have only given me half an hour at the end of which time they declare I must lunch with them which means I must take some whiskey and peppermint, which is the drink prescribed by the physicians, and it is more than up I will close. So Good bye my own dear wife. . . .

                                        Alfred

7

* * * * * * * * *

Toward the end of June, 1864, Captain Hough had an interview with General Thomas in which it was revealed that the latter had not been entirely blind to the conduct of Captain Young. Hough was now informed that his alcoholic superior was being relieved of his duties and that he would succeed to the position. He was directed to return to Nashville, pick up the records, and return to Chattanooga. On July 1 he could write his wife that he was now the Commissary of Musters for the Department of the Cumberland.

> Head-Quarters Department
> of the Cumberland
> Office Ass't Commissary of Musters,
> Chattanooga July 1 1864

My Dearest Wife

I arrived here yesterday and leave for Nashville today. I am now Com of Musters for the Dept, and am on my way to Nashville to relieve Capt Young and will then remove the office to this place Am now looking for quarters, so as to have everything ready, before I move down. I am very well but awful dirty, not having changed clothing since leaving Nashville. I have a great deal to say but have no time now, will write to you from Nashville. Was present at the assault on Monday, it was a desperate affair but unsuccessful.[1] Our loss is nearly 2000 with a great proportion of officers. The army is now trying another flank movement. . . . Good-bye love to the children as ever your true husband

Alfred L. Hough

HEAD-QUARTERS DEPARTMENT
OF THE CUMBERLAND
Office Commissary of Musters
Chattanooga July 1864

My Dearest Mary

Hot sweltering and dusty it is here now, yet I am well fixed, have an entire house for my office, everything is now unpacked and the work fairly under way, a few days more and all will be in order, of course much is new to me, and I am constantly busy. I have a room separate from my office for sleeping, and am in an old established mess, and this I think will be my home for many long weary months. I shall go to the front occasionally, but this is my Post. Much work is before me, and I shall give it all attention. My appointment gives satisfaction to all parties apparently, and shall endeavor not to disappoint them. Everything looks well at our front our army is now before Atlanta and in a few days

[1] He refers to the battle at Kenesaw Mountain on June 27. "I was with the General [Thomas] on a hill in full view during the attack and it was most distressing to see our poor fellows fall in front of the rifle pits, many of them on the enemys works when they fell, some of them falling inside and all without avail. As the General removed his glass from his eyes and started to leave the position we had just occupied, he said to me 'just as I expected' and not another word for some time." Alfred Lacey Hough, Manuscript Autobiography. See also Van Horne, op. cit, 232-236.

I fully believe it will be ours. What will be done then I know not but I have no doubt the Dept of Cumb proper will remain on this line, while McPherson will move elsewhere perhaps, Mobile, or perhaps to Army of Potomac. . . . Grant *must* succeed. I have very little fear on account of the raid near Baltimore. I have too much confidence in the patriotism of *some* of the people at home, they may do a great deal of damage to private parties, but Grant wont detach a man I am satisfied. I am disgusted though at the panic evinced by the people, it is shameful. . . . write often and remember me as ever your true husband

Alfred

HEAD-QUARTERS
DISTRICT NASHVILLE,
Office Commissary Musters,
Nashville, Tenn., July 3rd, 1864

My Own Dear Wife

After a long and tiresome ride I am again in Nashville well in health only suffering from fatigue. I am thankful it is only that for I have escaped accident where accidents have been around me. . . . Let me give you a brief history of my travels. I left here just three weeks since direct for Chattanooga where I arrived without accident with comparative comfort, remained two days visited Lookout and had a "view" taken (which I sent by mail for your disposal. I send you all of them). I then went to Huntsville, and staid one day busy all the time, this place I described to you two years since. I left the army then to rejoin you at Indianapolis, thence I went to Columbia, here I intended stopping some days with my friend Capt Hosea A. C. M. as it is a most delightful spot, and a number of intelligent Union people reside there, living in fine houses who entertain hospitably. But no sooner had I sat myself down for a little pleasure, when I received the despatch ordering me to the front. I was off at once, reached Chattanooga in 20 hours after a weary ride stopped all night, and then to Big Shanty on top of a freight car (no passenger cars on this road) mixed in with a lot of "bounty jumpers" under guard just out of prison covered with vermin, rode all day under a burning sun, was fired into by Guerillas, but only one man hurt crawled secretly into a car (against orders) for the night and slept on some amunition [sic] boxes, reached Big Shanty next day at noon, six miles to camp, and found plenty of work to do. Headquarters was overrun with business about mustering which they did not understand. I straightened them up and by the time I finished an answer to Genl Thomas' application came from Washington appointing me Chf Com of Musters for the Dept in place of Capt Young. While here nothing was done in the line of fighting except an assault by a portion of our line on the enemy's centre which failed. We lost about 2000 killed wounded and missing in about an hour, among them many officers. Our Division was not in it. I was with the General in our works during the assault, and though much whistling of iron was heard none of us were hit, this failure not unexpected, will cause another flank movement to be made. The enemy are strongly fortified at every position capable of it, and though we have driven them from line after line, we have got to continue it till they are worn out, both armies are gradually decreasing, but the end must come soon but yet with much loss to both. After completing the work at the front and giving them a fresh start, I was ordered to proceed to Nashville, relieve Capt Young, and remove the office to Chattanooga. I found the trains all loaded with sick and wounded but succeeded in getting on the regular hospital train as a special favor, this is fitted up for carrying the worst cases, with cooking apparatus and &c. I reached Chattanooga in safety in one day, only being harassed by the distress of the sufferers here let me give my testimony to good done by the Sanitary Commission, everything needful is supplied by them, and stations are established at different points along the road for supplying those not on regular hospital trains. I was amused at one poor fellow with one arm off, as the agent at Resaca was offering coffee and biscuits to them he replied "By thunder, I don't want anything, this is a hotel we are in, they shove grub into you every five minutes". Here let me say that on my trip down my train was the only one that got in for three days, the one before it was captured and burned, and a bridge was burned behind ours. But to resume, stopping one day at Chattanooga I started up again the train being mostly of sick and wounded the train before us was thrown off an embankment crushing the cars to pieces, wounding many but killing none; we were detained 28 hours behind time, and I arrived safely at last, tired and weary, the poor passengers suffering though by the delay; here again I saw the advantages of the Sanitary stations on the road. Tomorrow I shall relieve Capt Young and proceed to pack up for Chattanooga. In all this trip I have had no change of clothing, and have scarcely had my clothes off, when I was not travelling, I was working. It has been fully as wearisome as my field campaigns, but a good bath and a "biled" [white] shirt has made me feel quite fresh. . . . I am fast getting disgusted at the people at home, as is the whole army if they do not do something soon there will be trouble it is fearful to contemplate how quietly they sit at home "marrying and giving in marriage" while we are fighting *every man* in the rebel states. If we do not finish the matter this summer they *must* come, and will be forced to, this is my prediction. Just to think of our Congressmen sitting there afraid to repeal the exemption clause for fear they will not be re-elected, by their stay-at-home votes, while the President, the Sect of War, the Pro Marshal Genl, every military man in Congress, and thousands upon thousands of officers in the Army tell them that we cannot keep up our armies, and thoroughly break up this rebellion unless we have more men, and $300 is not a man. But the time will come, it will come, we have not fought for three years and seen our best friends and comrades fall around us for nothing. God grant that their eyes may be opened in time before they force anarchy upon the country, only to be removed through more blood. You ask me what I think of Grant's campaign. I think it most skilful and successful, and could only have been accomplished by a great man. Give him a 100,000 more men and what could he not do, and let a 100,000 men land near Mobile, and what could we not do here, and yet these people sit idly by and let us perish man by man, never thinking it is their duty to help but offer money as if that would suffice. No, they have bought all the substitutes they can, the supply is stopped, and now if we fail they must come, and when you have an opportunity let them know it. It will be sad times when an armed guard patrols every quiet hamlet among our once peaceful honest—but I am getting to lecturing. I always warm up on this subject.

You ask can't I come home? No dearest I have too much work here now. I shall be very very busy for months to come. Next winter if I live is the nearest I can hope for, after the '61 troops are mustered out. Genl Thomas has highly honored me, and I shall ask no favors, to lose thereby his good opinions, he has never left his post since the war began.

. . . Well good-bye all love to all, dear Mary my own true wife I am your loving husband

Alfred

HEAD-QUARTERS DEPARTMENT
OF THE CUMBERLAND
Office Commissary of Musters
Chattanooga July 17th 1864

My Dearest Wife

I have no letter from you since my last, and if I don't get one to-day I shall hardly expect one for some time, nor can I reasonably expect you will get this at the proper time. And for the same reason this letter will be a formal one that neither you nor I should object to having published in the rebel papers for curious eyes to gloat over. A large force of rebel cavalry crossed the Tennessee River some 60 miles below here on the 13th we have not heard from them since, but no doubt they will make a raid on our rear, and stop communication for a time, they cannot hurt us however, as they will be driven out and communication established again before we are in Nauton. All goes on well here, our army is now in front of Atlanta, a battle will no doubt be fought, and perhaps a siege have to be made but we shall take Atlanta, and until then I can make no calculations as to my movements, at present I am wanted here. I have much to do but at the present I shall be equally wanted at the front, but of one thing I can rest assured I shall have no idle time during this year.

We hear nothing at all from Grant lately, all the news we get is about the raid in Maryland I only sincerely trust it will again arouse our people and be the means of filling up the ranks of our armies. We have accomplished much very much, and if we could but increase our armies *now* we could accomplish all.

A veteran European soldier would be amazed should he travel over the route of our army from here to Atlanta 130 miles through a constant series of defences, mountains and rivers supported by the labor of thousands for months. The same thing could be said I suppose of the entire army, and now for the great struggle we have depleted ranks, plenty to hold what we have but can we do more? without assistance? that is the great question. The work must be done if it takes years, but how much better that it be done at once, and it could be so easily if our people would but do their duty. We have had dreadfully hot weather, and as I sit almost gasping for air, and look up at the peak of Lookout, how I long to be there. I have not been up since being here this time, but I understand the hospitals there are very complete, and all are comfortable. General Cruft is up there just recovering from a severe attack of fever as soon as I can get time I shall take a trip up and spend a night. Chattanooga proper is but a sorry place for a residence at this time, and I should think at any time in the summer months: We are surrounded by hills and the sun pours down on us terribly. We have no shade trees, all having been cut down for fire wood last winter, but I have a good house to protect me from the sun both for office and quarters, and at night I sleep sound after my day's work. I took a little ride after sunset for exercise, but it is too hot to go far.

By means of the sanitary garden we live well on vegetables, and I am very much more comfortable than ever before, I only wish my companions near Atlanta were but half so, but I must withhold my sympathies for myself, as I may very soon be with them, and Atlanta is said to be a very hot place. I have left Mr. Hays at Nashville, he will attend to all business there, and as his stay is likely to be a long one he will no doubt send for his wife. . . . Remember me to the family with all love to the children I remain as ever your own

Alfred

Chattanooga Tenn
July 24th 1864

Dearest Mary

. . . We have no official news from the front, and what we get from passengers all of whom are from the rear of our line is conflicting; that we are immediately in front of Atlanta is certain, also that our gallant army is fighting bravely with all prospect of success, but with what loss we cannot say, but most likely with very great. I hear of some of my friends. Genl McPherson's body has just arrived, this is a most serious loss, he was a man and a soldier; that the rebel army is fighting desperately you may know from Johns[t]on's being relieved because he said he could not hold Atlanta. Hardee refused the command for the same reason. [General John B.] Hood then accepted it, and said he could hold it, this is what is said by rebel prisoners (officers). Of course under the circumstances Hood will fight most desperately. I have however no doubt about the result, but we must pay for it with the blood of the best men of the country. When I think of all this, and hear of the dastardly apathy of the people who sent these noble men here to fight for their liberties, it is indeed disheartening. John writes me that the people are getting tired of the war, because it costs too much! Costs them too much? Yes, money! filthy money! I have long defended our people of the North from accusations made against them by officers returning from visits home, but I can do so no longer, they are creating a great gulf between us, acting as though they were the people, and we merely their hired soldiery paid fully for our labors, and at their will when they wish to economize, they will discharge us, and what remains of the noble army will turn their backs upon the graves of their late companions, leaving them to be desecrated by the rebels that slew them, and then crawl humbly home, to thank their employers. Oh how little they understand either us, or them themselves. *We* with the few that still stand firm at home are the *people* and will wield the destinies of the country for the future. There is fully as much virtue, and more ability in this army than in the same number of people who have held back. Let them know the truth that the brains of this country is now in the army, and they will be the traders. If they at home, refuse further supplies of men and means, the people, the real people, will not only do the fighting but the voting for the rest of the war. We are doing the thinking now, and there is but one feeling that of firm resolution to complete what has been begun and that fully and completely.

. . . Good bye with all the love you could wish I am your faithful husband

Alfred

HEAD-QUARTERS DEPARTMENT
OF THE CUMBERLAND
Office Commissary of Musters
Chatt. Wed July 27/64

My Dearest Mary

. . . I see by the *Northern papers* that we are in possession of Atlanta I am right glad to hear such good news and hope you fully enjoyed it. How this world is given to lying. We are not yet in possession. We have Atlanta much the same as Grant has Richmond, we have fought our way to the place and are now lying around one side of it endeavoring to starve them out. I have no doubt we will succeed they have made several attempts to drive us off every time with great loss to themselves and much loss to us. Our army has a month's supplies up with them and the communication of *250 mile*s yet fully open just think of that. I have no idea they have as much food as we have, and not as good prospects of keeping up the supply. I again assert although Atlanta is strongly fortified, we will soon have it.

I send you a photograph of Genl McPherson [killed in the Battle before Atlanta], it is a most excellent likeness, we mourn over his loss very much, there are some Generals whose ability we only admire, who have nothing in their character or demeanor that is particularly attractive, such a man is Sherman. There are others, who we not only respect for their ability but love for their goodness as men such a man was McPherson. Alas he is gone, one more tribute for the welfare of all of us. I wrote you the other day who my companions were in the picture on Lookout, and spoke of Col. Baemens always being wounded, he was again wounded in the fight before Atlanta last week, a bullet in his arm. I

should have finished this page but here comes Capt
[John] Rziha [19th Infantry] who will talk me tired,
so will close. Good bye as ever your husband

                                                Alfred

                  HEAD-QUARTERS DEPARTMENT
                  OF THE CUMBERLAND
                  Office Commissary of Musters
                  Chattanooga Aug 10/64

My Dearest Mary

. . . Your letter describing the state of public opinion only confirms what I have been thinking for some
time. That is that the people at home would prefer to
submit to the Rebel rather than come and help us fight.
And that if we do not achieve decisive victories before
Election day a new government will be inevitable which
will give them peace at any sacrifice. Well so mote [sic]
it be; but may God in his infinite mercy prevent such a
catastrophe as the latter. You need not expect to hear
of victories. We must have more men first. We shall
not fail at Atlanta, But Grant will fail *for the present*
at Richmond and if that lack of success should cause the
formation of a new government, good bye to peace and
a quiet home for all *our time* this is my firm belief and
oh how the idea harasses me. A declaration of the government to have peace would no more cause peace until
the cause of the war was taken away, than my "declaration" would carry an assault. And what are we poor
soldiers to do in this case, can we who really feel what
we are fighting for, and now have the additional incen-
tive of pride to carry us on, quietly skulk away to our
homes? No! we must fight on through our whole lives
for principle. Oh it fairly makes me sick to think of it.
If Mr. Lincoln and a supporting Congress are elected

this fall, I can see the end of the war during his Administration. If *any other* person with supporting Congress is elected I can see nothing but anarchy, a long war and eventually a dismembered country, of all of which my destiny is to be a part of. God grant there may be wisdom enough left among your people for them to see their own weakness, and that the very cowardice and selfishness of the creatures may induce them to take the right step.

I intended after my last letter on public affairs to say no more on the subject, but I cannot help it especially when you give me such an excellent text. I will endeavor not to for the future, for the idea of this continual separation is becoming more and more dreadful to bear. God bless you and our little ones. . . . With all love, dearest,

Alfred

Chattanooga Sept. 5th 1864

My Dearest Mary:

. . . I am entirely convalescent, and only lack a little strength to be entirely well. I am not attending to business yet, but am resting and enjoying a good appetite the weather is very delightful now, and tomorrow I intend going on to Lookout Mountain to spend a few days and then return to business. I am satisfied it is all for the best that I did not get started for home, but if it had not been for this rebel cavalry I should have been there by this time. In the first place my services are *needed* here, and knowing that as anxious as I am to be with you I should have been harassed about business all the time I was gone, and most likely have felt it my duty to have resigned my position, which I would dislike to do very much, not only because it is pleasant but because my services the next two months will I think entitle me to considerable credit "with the powers that be", as I know I am giving real satisfaction to the troops that are going out of service and then when I do see you I want to be well, and enable us both to have some enjoyment from our union. Another objection to my going now is the pending election I don't want to be in the excitement of it, I am so much disgusted with so many of my old friends. . . . Our war news here is most gratifying we have Atlanta, but no particulars of it yet whether a fight or evacuation we don't know. And the rebel raid so far has been a failure. They commenced a little north of Atlanta and have been driven from every point on the road they have attacked till they have reached Nashville where they are now, and even if they should succeed in breaking the road *north* of here for *three months* it would make no difference to us, only a little annoyance, and *north* of us we are good for a month, and trains are rushing down supplies from here very fast constantly. We have the Democratic platform, and even the McClellan men are disgusted, if the people north should elect a man on such a platform, they deserve to be slaves, and our time as nation will be short. . . . as ever your true husband

Alfred

Chattanooga Sept 10th 1864

My Dearest Mary:

We have the first train through from Nashville today with a week's mail, and not a letter from you, it has been now *such* a long time since I heard from you, but I have no doubt there were letters for me and they have gone on to Atlanta with the rest of Hd quarter's mail. [General Joseph] Wheeler has sadly interfered with our mails and newspapers, but that is about all I believe; he has captured no trains or stores and the road has been repaired as fast as he tore it up. I believe he is getting away now as fast as he can with considerable less number of men than he brought with him. . . . I am off for Atlanta on Monday next. The whole of Hd Qrs office is ordered there, which is to be permanent Hd qrs and right glad I am of it, this is a most awful place terribly dull and everybody sick. I hear we have fine quarters selected, the climate is fine, and then I shall be with all my old friends, and cheerful company is what I want, for although I am apparently well I am yet a little weak and dare not trust my head to regular work or reading, and as there is nobody to talk to it is most horribly dull here. . . . I can get a leave at any time because I have declined the one just offered me. My Doctor tells me that going to Atlanta is just the very next best thing to going home, the change will do me great good, and besides I know myself that when I get my office to Atlanta right at Hd Quarters, I can put another officer in charge of it which I could not do here and leave with much less responsibility on my mind. Our campaign is ended for some months anyhow. The army is to be reorganized, &c. and *ought* to be reinforced before we attempt anything further. I *hope* you wont elect McClellan but *expect* you will and what will be done I can only surmise "Peace at any price" I suppose, and the old state of affairs over again. I suppose the draft is now going on and you have rebellion at home, well you must put it down, or else we will have to stop fighting the rebels here at present and turn our attention to our friends at home. We are sending all the troops whose time expires soon, home very fast, especially to Indiana God grant we may pass through this election calmly and quietly if so, and Lincoln is re-elected by a decided majority I can see light ahead, but otherwise all is dark to me, and I dare not think of the future, either of my country or my family. . . . I am as ever your true and loving husband

Alfred

Atlanta Georgia Sept 16, 1864 [2]

My Own Dear Wife

. . . I am now unpacked, office arranged, and every thing in working order, have worked off the unfinished business waiting for me, and last evening mounted my horse and took a view of the city. . . . I am now perfectly well, and am enjoying this delightful climate with all the zest of a healthy man, work, study, eat heartily and sleep soundly. . . . I have been interrupted four times since I commenced this letter and now have not time to say half that I wanted to about Atlanta and the army. It may be only temporary but the climate of this country is delightful, a fine breeze is stirring all the time, which prevents the sun from being oppressive, and the nights are so beautiful Oh what nights for sleeping. The place itself is solid and business like, wide streets and many fine houses. The dwelling part of the city looks like a prosperous western town, and the business part like Philadelphia or New York. The army is resting and everybody appears to be enjoying them-

[2] Hough's Autobiography supplies the information that he arrived at Atlanta on the night of September 12 "with my train of 10 cars of office furniture, records, clerks, orderlies, etc. Next morning I found my old friends in peaceful possession of Atlanta and glad to see me, General Thomas taking dinner time for an opportunity of discussing business, asked me to dine with him, after which he gave me the necessary instructions. I was soon established in a house in Atlanta, and my clerks at work, and then had an opportunity of seeing the city and the effects of the siege."

selves. Many people were left here, but they are to go,
—in my next I will tell you about them. I must now
close and bid you good bye. . . .

Your husband
Alfred

Atlanta Ga. Sept 18th 1864

My Dearest Mary

We have a drizzling rain to-day which makes our
new city look somewhat gloomy, but still if I could hear
church bells ringing to-day would seem like Sunday in
a Northern city. I still keep well, and have had a fair
opportunity of seeing the city, living in Atlanta must
have been anything but pleasant for the last few weeks
(previous to our entry) About one half of the city show
the marks of our shells, the house we mess in has five
holes through it, the one I live in has only one some
houses are perfectly riddled. Almost every house has
what we call a "gopher hole" attached to it, that is a
large hole made in the yard, then covered with timber
and the earth that came out of the hole thrown over
the timber, with a small entrance to it on the *south* side
small holes are left for ventilation. Many of these have
been nicely fixed up with furniture and stoves in them.
The one in my yard has bunks fixed along the sides and
is very comfortable. The people lived in these during
the shelling, and our officers tell me they found these
"gopher holes" all through the country between here
and Jonesboro where the battle was fought that gave
us Atlanta thirty miles south. Our men taunted the
rebel prisoners with their fear of us, telling them "to
go in their holes", they always attempted to explain
that the women built them. We found about one fourth
of the population remaining in Atlanta, but very few

able bodied young men and what there were had been working in the Govt shops a good many foreigners, many poor people, and some of the upper class, but no negroes except old ones Sherman's order to depopulate the place created some excitement at first, but they are satisfied of the necessity of it, when they came to understand that there was no means of feeding them. All who want to go south can go, and all go north that want to. They have the privilege of taking a small quantity of furniture, and are allowed to sell all they can. Many officers (who have money) have fixed themselves up nicely. This will be strictly a military Post no non-combatants other than Govt employes will be allowed, even the usual camp followers who have kept in the rear during the campaign are not allowed to come up. I do wish you could just drop in on us, the ladies do look so queer to me, none of them have crinoline, and the styles of dress are numerous. There is most excellent order in the city the inhabitants are well pleased with our conduct and say openly they are better protected personally than they were by the rebel army. You must read Sherman and Hood's correspondence I suppose it will be in the Northern papers. We have had a flag of truce for ten days for delivery of the citizens and for a *special* exchange of prisoners it ends to-day. The supposition is the campaign will not open again for about six weeks. A great many leaves and furloughs are being given, and a general fixing up going on. The army is in excellent spirits and only waiting for reinforcements to fill up the places of those we are mustering out. We all want the draft. Sherman telegraphed the President that if the draft was not fully enforced he need not expect a vote in the army; the greatest subject of conversation and argument is that Genl Thomas "Old Pop" as they call him has sent for his wife to come and see him, he has not seen her since the war commenced, and can't find time to go and see her. You have no idea how he is beloved by the army. Sherman is admired and respected as an able man, but Thomas is beloved in addition. I have not been among the troops any yet they are all in the works outside of town, but shall take a general survey in a few days. I have seen some of the works and find them unusually strong. They never expected Atlanta would be taken. Oh only give us another army *now* and we will soon finish the war. . . . As ever your true husband,

Alfred

Atlanta, Georgia
Sept 21st 1864

My Dearest Mary

I am driving away hard at work as usual. I really do not know how they would have got along without me. There are all sorts of questions arising about the muster out of men. And as I have made it a specialty everything depends upon my decision. So if I am not gaining any ability I have the satisfaction of knowing I am doing the Govt some service. But I have great satisfaction in knowing that my services are appreciated and withal I am very well satisfied.

I am very well and if I only had a little more time to go round and see the army should really enjoy myself, but between talking and writing I can only steal an hour or so a day for a short ride. Consequently I can tell you no more of Atlanta than I did in my last. Everything is going on as usual, very quiet but preparations being made for another campaign. Leaves and furloughs are being given freely, and unless the Rebs move on our communications we are likely to have a quiet time for some weeks. To be sure we don't live very well, as no transportation is allowed to sutlers and we get very little beyond army food, but plenty of that. We manage to get a few things though for change but at an immense cost. But we make up for it in having good houses to live in, and the appearance of civilization around us. The city is fast becoming purely military most of the citizens have left, but some manage to remain, and as the truce ends to-day, I suppose what are here now will stay and be employed by the Govt and private parties in various ways; none of the wealthy remain. The houses on the outskirts of the city are being torn down to furnish lumber for the soldiers' huts,[3] and I could not but think of how little these people knew what war would be when they commenced it. I witnessed a spectacle a few days since. A long train of ambulances filled with women and children with a *few* very old and young men or boys, followed by wagons filled with furniture was passing out of the city toward the rebel lines and on each side of them were a detachment of soldiers de-

[3] "A line or irregular circle had been determined upon for our interior line of defense; outside of this circle were many houses, some of them fine dwellings. About 8 o'clock in the morning the troops were notified that they could take any lumber or other material from these houses that they might need to make huts of, as they were to be torn down. Before sunset every vestige of these houses, except the mortar that had fallen from the bricks, was gone. An equally effective establishment of property was then made, for before another 24 hours had passed, long rows of comfortable huts were to be seen, all made of the material from these houses. It was a sad sight to look upon the long trains of wagons with the loads of women and children and furniture passing out of the city toward the Rebel lines, under the order of depopulation referred to, but it was necessary." Alfred Lacey Hough, Manuscript Autobiography.

molishing their houses and casting off the lumber. We are fast increasing the population of Southern Georgia with women, children, old men and negroes Such is war, may you never witness it. . . .

I am getting along with my work so well and getting things arranged so completely that I *may* get home before December. Consequently I am anxious to know where I will find you. I have had no letters since my last and am anxiously looking for some. We are in good spirits to-day over a reputed victory by Sheridan. I hope it is all true. Genl Thomas says the "rebellion is tottering" which is a great deal for him to say. . . . as ever your true husband

Alfred

Atlanta Ga., Sept 23, 1864

My Dearest Mary

I have no letter from you since my last and am dreadfully homesick for one. The mails are very much deranged now in consequence of the constant attacks of the rebels on our line of communication. They are making every effort to prevent us from bringing up supplies and not a day passes that a train is not attacked or the road torn up. We have to keep a large force to watch and repair, and yesterday quite a number of troops were sent to the rear to meet a large force that has gone into Tennessee. So altogether the mails are very doubtful, and appearances are not much in favor of an early campaign. Atlanta will likely be a resting place for some time, but no rest for the staff Depts all are busy refitting and consolidation now going on will give me plenty to do all the time. All this speculation is conditional upon the rebels not attacking us. They may do that, and we have reports they are being reinforced for the purpose but I don't believe it. Consequently we are living a very quiet business like life, the weather is delightful and I am really enjoying the climate. I have never been so forcibly impressed with the advantages of a good climate as I have been here, perhaps it is because I have been sick and vividly feel the change in my condition, but everybody speaks of it. I am very well now and do not experience any fatigue from labor, but enjoy a hard ride after a day's work in the office, but I do not get my color back (what little I had). I am pale and thin and begin to look old so you will have no need to complain of my youthful looks for the future. We get very few papers now and what we get are a week old nearly so with the exception of despatches from Washington to Hd Qrs know very little of what is going on. We are now in receipt of great news from Sheridan which I trust is all true. From the tone of the papers we get though I should judge there was quite a reaction in favor of Lincoln. McClellan is fast losing what friends he had in the army and I have no doubt Lincoln will have a large majority of the army vote. The Chicago [peace] platform is more than our heroes can stand. Grant though must be getting all the recruits we hear of being obtained as none of them are coming to us. I sent you in my last two checks. . . . I hope you will get it safely and I only wish it was more. My pay seems like a poor pittance when we have privates coming down here who have received from $1000 to $2000 for enlisting as substitutes for *one year*. Thank God, my children will not have to say their father refused to go to the field when he was wanted. . . .

Your true husband
Alfred

Atlanta Oct 2d 1864

My Dearest Mary

This is my day for writing but as we are cut off entirely from the North, there is no use of starting a letter. I will however keep a diary writing on my regular days and when we have communication again make a final item and start it off. The rebels are making a desperate attempt to force us to retreat by massing on our rear. They some time since sent a large cavalry force into Tennessee which our troops have been fighting for some time; we sent two Divisions back there and Genl Thomas went back himself to attend to them. We hear nothing from them, but I suppose you do. Since then the entire rebel army have crossed the Chattahoochie and are moving on our line towards Marietta, to meet this Genl Thomas has started our army back, and they are now on the march, leaving only the 20th corps to hold Atlanta. Consequently we are now isolated entirely with a prospect of being so for some time. I suppose a battle will be fought north of us, and if our forces are worsted, we here have a "smart" chance of being gobbled. We have however plenty of food and amunition [*sic*] and will be found "hard to take". But alas for our mails I fear it will be a long time before we hear from each other again, and I am so very anxious to hear from you now.

I am very well and shall now have but little to do for a while, this movement of troops stopping work in my line. I shall proceed to hunt up a novel and take to heavy reading, this startling us from our preparations is anything but pleasant, it prevents us from preparing for another campaign, prevents our army from being paid, and stops things generally, and if we should get whipped would be very bad indeed, if however we should beat them it will give us a clean sweep of this part of the Confederacy—"so moot it be".

A.

Oct. 5th 1864

No Change in the state of affairs since my last excepting we now know that one corps and some cavalry of the rebels are left in our front; whether they intend to attack us or not we cannot tell; but we are getting ready to receive them, making an interior line of defences enclosing the depots and storehouses and high part of the town. The lines runs between my office and dwelling house leaving the latter just outside which will be torn down and we now see the wisdom of Sherman's idea of sending the families away. A great many are yet here and will be sadly in our way if we are attacked. If we are not attacked before three days, all of Hood's army cannot take us. We hear nothing from the rear and do not know whether any fighting is going on or not. Our principal topic of conversation is planning for the future. We have food for several months by good management, though very little meat. We will have to go it on hard bread. Our horses will have to be killed before many weeks as we have no forage, and again if the rebel army should succeed in forcing our army back, we speculate upon the chances of our marching through to Pensacola. This is all based upon the possibility of rebel successes, but it is astonishing how confident we have become. Not a man doubts our being able to foil their intentions. It is however very annoying not to hear anything either from home or the army. I fear you are worried about me as no doubt you will have all sorts of rumors, and I dread to think of how long it may be before I hear from you. The whole army is intensely

anxious to hear from other scenes of the war, as the last
news we had showed a very active time with Grant and
Sheridan also in Missouri. . . . Good bye for to-day

A.

Oct 9th 1864

Dearest:

A week has rolled around since I commenced this, a
week of anxiety, but the crisis is passed. We have foiled
Hood completely in his attempted imitation of Sherman's movement on Atlanta. He threw a whole corps
on our sub-base at Altoona Pass, but before he could
get them all into action Sherman was on top of his
whole army with ours, and he was compelled to with-
draw all but one Division, which made desperate as-
saults but were repelled by the gallant garrison under
Genl Corse. The enemy lost about 1200 men and retired we lost heavy 600 out of about 2000 it was a most
desperate fight, but turned the scale Sherman quickly
drew Hood off the RR and he is now retiring having
accomplished nothing more than destroying some six
miles of RRoad which will be repaired in a week. The
Corps that was watching us, moved up around our
works but quickly retired after Hood's repulse. We
have no mails through yet, but the telegraph will be up
to-day, and then we can get some news from the North.
We hear reports that Forrest has done nothing in Tennessee, and that a great battle is being fought near
Richmond all of which we are anxiously waiting to hear
officially about. All this may not interest you dearest,
but you get the current of our thoughts. Shut up as we
have been and in fact are yet, you can imagine how
greedy we are to hear from "God's country". As to
private news we are [long?]ing dreadfully for it. We

have no hopes though of getting our mails till the road is repaired. The first person through from Altoona was one of my assistants, who started from Chattanooga a week since and got as far as the former place and was present at the fight. He arrived last night and had an audience of all our staff here at my room, he was the lion of the evening, and was most entertaining. A day or two more will develop whether Mr. Hood is going to continue his attempts to worry us, or whether we will be allowed to sit quietly awhile in Atlanta to get rested fed up and paid. We are anxiously looking for the return of the main body of the Army. As we have no newspapers, see nobody but ourselves, and no great accident or event has happened *in* Atlanta you now have my budget for to-day. I am only afraid this movement of the army will delay my visit home, as immediately upon the army getting in camp again, I will be overrun with business delayed by the movement. I want to go home next month if I can. But dearest Mary I am so well that I fairly jump sometimes with elation, this climate is so delightful. How fortunate for me to be sent away from Chattanooga.

                                                    Alfred

                                            Oct 11th 1864
Dearest
    The first mail starts for the North to-day and I hasten to close my letter. As soon as I heard last night that a mail was to start I wrote a short note and mailed it for fear I could not get this in in time. We are as yet very uncertain as to army movements. The rebels were defeated at Altoona and driven off the road but whether they intend to retreat or move to the North next and strike higher up we cannot tell, the appearances are

that they will try the latter if so our army will have to
move with them, leaving us isolated at Atlanta for
some time. But most likely in the latter case I shall go
with them as my business must be attended to and I
cannot wait for returns to come to Atlanta to be again
sent to Washington. So you *may* hear from me soon at
Chattanooga. Confound the rebels I fear this movement of them will delay my visit home as we can do
but little while the army is in motion, and I will be overrun when they come to a stop. How long it seems since
I heard from you, how many letters there must be on
the way for me. This is election day how quiet here and
how much excitement there must be with you. Good bye
my dearest God bless you and ours. May we soon meet
in happiness as ever your true and loving husband

Alfred

HEAD-QUARTERS DEPARTMENT
OF THE CUMBERLAND
Atlanta Oct 17th 1864

My dearest Mary

Another week has rolled around and still we are
blockaded. I sent off last Tuesday two sheets to you,
and at that time was under the impression the blockade
was raised and that we should have free communication, but we are disappointed. The Rebs have pushed
farther North our army following and what they are
doing now we have no idea, only that our army is nearer
Chattanooga than Atlanta. Whether my letters got
through or not I cannot tell but most sincerely hope so.
After we drove them off the road at Altoona we had
communication with Nashville for a day by telegraph.
I despatched Hays a message to write to you that I was
well I hope he got it, but before I could get any answer,

the Rebs were on the road again further up. The movements of the enemy are most incomprehensible. I cannot see anything for them but disaster, they cannot starve us out here unless they whip Sherman, and that is almost impossible. They have however delayed our campaign *from* here for some time to come. We were very fortunate however in getting a very large mail through from the north before they struck the road a second time it slipped through between the attacks, among others, *many* others for my brother officers were yours of 21st blowing me up for thinking McClellan would be elected and . . . your reproof for my despondency about public matters is most welcome and I am most happy to hear of the change of sentiment North, we have the same feeling here in the army. Lincoln will get almost the entire vote. We are now very anxious to hear from the State elections, and so much news yet for us to hear makes us long for a regular mail. I suppose you know by the papers what our army is doing while we are in total ignorance, rather a singular state of affairs.

We live on in the even tenor of our way, perfectly isolated from the rest of the world feeling perfectly secure. The enemy are afraid to attack us so far and every day we are more secure. We have plenty of rations, and have sent out two large foraging parties each bringing in 50 loads of forage for our horses, having a fight with cavalry both times. So altogether our lot is not so very hard after all but only most provoking. . . . And as for yourself I most fully recant my heresy about McClellan so that there need be no "trouble in the family". I do hope the next mail will bring more letters from you and ones that will tell me something about yourself, as these though very welcome were most concise and very foreign.

Good bye dearest God bless you and the children and may we soon meet in happiness.

Your husband
Alfred

Atlanta Oct 21/64

Dearest Mary

We have a despatch through from Nashville to-day, the first flash, telling us the elections have gone all right, of course we are in good spirits. Our army is still after Hood (or Beauregard?) off towards Alabama, and we are still without news from there. We are surrounded by cavalry who watch us close and pick up any stragglers who may wander outside of the pickets. No mail since my last, but are promised one tomorrow, the R road is promised to be finished in a week and then we hope to feel nearer home. Under the circumstances "we are as well as could be expected"; having no news, I will close, with all love.

Alfred

HEAD-QUARTERS DEPARTMENT
OF THE CUMBERLAND
Atlanta Oct 23d 1864

My Dearest Wife

I have yours of 9th inst Oh what welcome epistle for now I seem to be so much nearer "God's country"; it is so desolate to be cut off as we have been from all we love, but now the mails run regularly and I do not think we shall be cut off again now. Our army has not returned yet, and it may not come this way but strike south by another route, from Rome towards Montgomery as that is the direction the Rebels lay, but another week will tell. From the tone of the rebels papers and especially Jeff Davis' speech at Macon they must have expected wonders from Hood's movement on our rear, and how disappointed they must be for this very day cars can run through Nashville again. Genl Thomas is still in Nashville, but from appearances another campaign will soon commence. We have news this morning of another victory by Sheridan, how successful he has been and how rejoiced you all must be and from all we can hear the elections have gone all right too. The skies are certain brighter. . . . We still have delightful weather, and the mails coming in have given me work again, but during my idleness I learned the game of chess much to my satisfaction besides reading Pendennis; from this time out though I expect to be busy. My letters must be very flat and uninteresting, but really we have nothing to write about. We see nothing here but ourselves and one day is just like another, all of us thinking of home and those we love, and at this time waiting for letters and papers. . . . I remain your true husband

Alfred

HEAD-QUARTERS DEPARTMENT
OF THE CUMBERLAND
Chattanooga, Nov 2 1864

My Dearest Mary

I have arrived here to-day Our Head Quarters are now here have not written since last Wednesday as I have not had my clothes off since Thursday last, have been a whole week on the way, find five letters here from you two old ones and three recent the last Oct. 24th. Oh it is so good to hear so late from you. I am writing this on a box will write fully as soon as I get my office open. Genl Sherman is going to cut loose and go south. Genl Thomas has an independent army in the rear which accounts for our being here, everything is in confusion and so am I. With all love good bye

Alfred

Address here.

Chattanooga Nov 6th 1864

My Dearest Wife

I am at last after eight days confusion and turmoil fixed in my old quarters and again started in business. And as soon as I have "housecleaning" shall feel somewhat comfortable, but as my quarters were occupied by "American citizens of African descent" during my absence, they are decidedly more dirty than "out of doors". . . . You were no doubt surprised at hearing from me from this place, but we expected it some time before we were ordered. The way of it is this, Hood's attempt to cut off our communications and thereby cause us to retreat from Atlanta has utterly failed, but causes an entire change of the campaign. Hood has been driven off the Road but still is concentrated on the line north from Montgomery and intends striking for Tennessee. Genl Thomas comes back here with part of the army and with the addition of new troops will hold our old line, from Knoxville through this place to Huntsville and Decatur. Sherman with 50 or 60 thousand men, will cut *loose from Atlanta previously destroying it, and the Railroad from it some distance north and march south*. This is not official neither has it been announced, but we can tell the movements from the preliminary ones. By the time this reaches you perhaps you will hear the above, and the next time you hear from Sherman it will be from salt water. In the mean time we may have some hard fighting to keep Hood from marching north but we will do it, and of one thing you may be sure, if Mr. Hood keeps on his present plan while he is fighting us Sherman will make a black mark through the south, and you may hear from him before spring south of Richmond. If Hood concludes to go after Sherman why we will have a quiet time; Sherman will cut entirely loose with only sufficient train to forage off the country on which his army will subsist and for amunition [sic]. Part of our Dept goes with him and part remains with us we will have about 50000 men on this line with the new troops. If Hood attacks this line it will be from the west in which direction he appears to be going now. At present all is uproar and turmoil, officers and men from leave rushing to Atlanta and the sick and disabled, with extra stores artillery &c. coming this way 400 cars left here for Atlanta yesterday. Genl Thomas is in Nashville organizing the new troops and watching Hood from the centre of his operations. Since I commenced this letter a vast amount of business has poured in upon me, but I would not stop till I got through but I have now finished and will say Good bye . . .

Alfred

HEAD-QUARTERS DEPARTMENT
OF THE CUMBERLAND
Office Commissary of Musters
Chatt Nov 13th 1864
My Dearest Mary

This is Sunday evening and I am in my lonely old room having been gone all day on Lookout Mountain. I have been very busy all the week and had to take to-day to go up there to see the "Regulars" who are stationed there now, I had a very pleasant ride but feel awfully tired and shall go to bed and to a sound sleep as soon as I finish this. I am very well and very busy see and hear nothing but mustering and to-day was a great relief to me. . . . The grand movement has now commenced. We are cut loose from Atlanta, which is at last "evacuated" but not in the way the rebels hoped. Sherman with 50000 Infantry and 6000 cavalry has struck for salt water. Genl Thomas with (not quite) as many more is on this line, most of them near Pulaski while Hood is at Florence with his army, look on the map and you will see the situation. Without Hood leaves to follow Sherman, there will soon be a great battle between him and Thomas. In the mean time I can see nothing in Sherman's way without some very unforeseen accident will soon strike a terrible blow. How I long to hear from the Rebels about Sherman, what a mail there will be. I still expect to be with you in Lewisburg but I am afraid not much before Christmas. I am waiting to see Genl Thomas who will be here in about a week, but *if* he should say no! What would I do, but I guess it will all be right.

Genl Cruft is here in command of detachments but I have not seen him yet, his health is not good. We have had great relief at the result of the elections and now feel that though we may have a long war yet, our country has shown herself worthy of being a nation and will be. I have heard from nobody north since my last to you, but getting the paper as we do here takes off the loneliness we felt at Atlanta during the blockade. But this place is hopeful and especially so to me since I was sick here. But I see no relief for evidently this will be Genl Thomas' Hd quarters for a long time to come we never expect to see Sherman's army again. They will operate east while we hold this line and keep the rebels from going North. If we whip them badly we may push them but that is doubtful. . . . I am as ever your true husband

Alfred

Chattanooga Nov 20th 1864

My Dearest Mary

. . . You were no doubt surprised at my information about Sherman's movements, but they were only conjectures that have since been confirmed. As to his particular plans we are as much in the dark as you are, whether to Mobile, Charleston or Savannah. The general opinion appears to be to one of the latter, but I would not be surprised if to all, first to Mobile, and then by transports to the Atlantic, but by the time this reaches you, the rebel papers will have informed you. As to Hood he appears to be perfectly confounded; he has not dared to move from his position at Florence yet. Thomas is quietly waiting for him, and in the meantime all goes on as usual in this department; the mails are regular, and we cannot help comparing our position with that of a year ago, when we were here half starved, now we have plenty of everything, with as much force here as then and have sent 60000 men right into the heart of the Rebellion. How calmly the Copperheads have settled down since the election, you all appear to be as mild as new milk to use a homely expression, and to my astonishment I hear no complaint of frauds and military resistance of Democratic votes, &c. Everything looks well now, and if we can only keep up our financial system, before Mr. Lincoln's time expires we will have a restored Union, and future history will place Mr. Lincoln's name next to Washington;

The first the founder the second the preserver of our country.

I want you to keep up a good thinking between now and the time I get home, we must plan for the future although a soldier has but little reason to make such plans in time of war, as he holds life by such slight tenure, but still we must plan as though life were certain. If prices get no higher I suppose we can manage to live till better times, but all this we must canvass and when I return to the army from my leave, it will either be to remain permanently in the service, a soldier for life, or only for the purpose of resigning in order to enter into some business that will support myself and family in the manner we have been used to living. I do not want to leave the service, I like it, the only drawback to my perfect content is the absence of my family, but that I have no right to expect in time of war, and in more peaceful times we can be together. But after four years of service my conscience will free me from further obligations if my family need me elsewhere. I write this now because I want us to have a free and full discussion when we meet and then decide finally and stand by the decision let what will come.

I have no interesting news, we have sent north all the refugees and sick and Chattanooga has settled down into quiet, a large garrison well supplied and strongly fortified, containing all the surplus baggage of our armies, it is an important place and if Mr. Hood should decide to want it he would be *warmly* received, and if we are not swallowed up in mud before spring, next year will be the beginning of a new era for this place. Good bye love to all, as ever your true husband

Alfred

Chattanooga Nov 27th 1864

My Dearest Mary

I wrote you a hurried note yesterday to send by a passenger going north by the only train that I felt pretty certain would get through, I don't feel entirely certain that he will but hope. I shall entrust this to the hazards of the mail through the Rebel Cavalry.

Before the time this should reach you, you will most likely know more about matters than I will but at this time we are about in the following situation, and with the news you get from the papers if this should get through, you will have a pretty good idea of our condition if you should not hear from us for some time.

Genl Thomas has withdrawn from Pulaski and is concentrating his army nearer Nashville I *suppose* on our old line at Murfreesboro, holding the line from there to Franklin, which will compel Hood to fight him some 100 miles from his base without Railroad communication, and if Hood does go on to him there, I predict he will be badly beaten.

I am particular in this description, because there is nothing contraband if the Rebels should capture this as they know all that is herein contained. But of our situation I can say nothing, only that you need have no fear of us, we can stay here and save all our positions until such time as the Rebels shall be driven south again, but until that is done we fully expect to be cut off from the main army. We may be and most likely will be attacked, but we have enough both of food for ourselves and amunition [*sic*] for our enemies. In the meantime we have the first rumors of Sherman's progress both from northern papers and from refugees, and we can well permit Hood to ravage Tennessee where he will hurt his friends more than ours when by that Sherman will have a clean sweep till he meets troops from the east, and every man that opposes him now must weaken Lee that much. You now have a schedule of the whole condition, and personally I am about as usual. The Head-quarters of the Dept are still here, and as soon as this raid of Hood's is stopped all will come back, and then and not till then can I go home. I am afraid I shall not get home as soon as I expected, but such are the uncertainties of war. . . .

Alfred

HEAD-QUARTERS DEPARTMENT
OF THE CUMBERLAND
Office Commissary of Musters
Chattanooga Dec 15th 1864

My Dearest Mary:

I have not written to you for nearly three weeks, how long a time it seems, but there has been no opportunity of sending a letter, it was therefore useless to write. If we had been experiencing an interesting or eventful life I might have written as usual and given you a history of our doings, to be read when they could be sent you, but it has been decidedly to the contrary, a most dull and monotonous time we are having, not even an attack from the rebels to excite us. How much longer this is to continue I cannot say but I fear many weeks yet. Genl Thomas does not seem disposed to attack Hood, but still keeps on the defensive at Nashville. Well we must wait in patience I suppose, but it is very hard on me, I had so impressed myself with the idea of spending Christmas with you, that my disappointment is almost like a child's. I can almost cry with vexation.

If I were busy it would tend to relieve me, but I am cut off entirely from my business, and it is accumulating against me to be done hereafter I have telegraphed another officer to act for me at Nashville, but only a portion of it can be attended to by him. We have still communication with the North and Nashville by the way of Knoxville and Louisville, but that is broken every day or two so we get but little news, the last we have is four days old which says Sherman is near Savannah so that is some comfort. If he will only send back one corps here we can drive back these Rebels, but we have one consolation they are only weakening themselves by this movement. They have done us no injury as yet we have the road open from here to Murfreesboro, and they have not captured any stores or permanent positions from us, nor do I think they will. They must go back sooner or later and their whole movement will only amount to a raid. . . . I am very well, but getting gray! not much to be sure, but they are straggling in gradually, but this you will be glad of no doubt. Well we are certainly getting old, but enough of that.

Besides the talk of and waiting for war news, we have had a little ripple of interest in the narratives of adventures of escaped prisoners. Some 40 of our officers have come on here having escaped from Columbia, S. C. Among them is Capt [Verling K.] Hart of our Regiment; their accounts are very interesting all of which I can tell you of some long evening when we are "together" We also have fearful tales of Refugees who are driven from their homes and come to us for protection. I have witnessed some harrowing scenes and have seen some *ladies* with their children, that made me think of my dear ones, people who had lived in affluence apparently, without a cent of money or food to eat. We take care of all who come the best we can Oh it is terrible. May you never experience it, or even see it. . . . Good bye God bless you all with sincere love I remain

Your true husband

Alfred

Chatt. Dec. 20th 1864

My Dearest Mary

Old "Tom" has cleaned out Hood and a messenger starts immediately from here to join him. I send this letter by him in haste I am very well With all love I am your true husband

Alfred

Chattanooga Tenn
Christmas Morn. 1864

Let the heavens rejoice, and let the earth be glad; let the sea roar, and the fulness thereof. Let the fields be joyful, and all that is therein; then shall the trees of the wood rejoice.[4]

My Dearest Mary:

This is the manner of our feeling this morning, and has been for the last 24 hours, yesterday we received our first mail and what a Christmas eve we had, and what a Christmas day we are having. A whole month blockaded, and then on Christmas eve to have our

[4] Hough relates in his autobiography that full particulars of the victory at Nashville arrived on Christmas Eve which made it a very happy holiday for those waiting at Chattanooga. "Indeed I never spent a more delightful Christmas week, the strain that had been upon us was now relaxed, for we did sometimes have visions of rebel prison pens; we had received no letters for a month and now we expected numbers. We had numerous reunions among the Officers and wound up with another great dinner party at General [Thomas Francis] Meaghers at which he shone brilliantly with his Irish wit and humor."

homes opened up to us by sweet letters from them, and
papers bringing us the details of our glorious victory
here, and good news from everywhere. Let us all rejoice. Oh it is hard that I am not at home, but all happiness is comparative and as compared with our recent
life this day is glorious. I have four letters from you
the last one dated 9th inst. You do not seem yet to
realize that I could not be with you but fear it, poor
soul, how disappointed you must have been when you
first did realize it. Well it can't be helped such is the
fortune of war. And I only hope you may have heard
or seen something to enable you to spend a happy
Christmas without me; for indeed dearest I must be
honest and confess that much as I was disappointed at
not getting home, and much as I suffered till yesterday,
when the mail did come and I got your letters and the
newspapers I was happy very happy and a right jolly
party were at my room last night, and a right good
Christmas dinner we are going to have as soon as I
finish your letter. After reading my Bible a while this
morning I took a long ride, and drank some excellent
egg nogg and after dinner I hope to have a good smoke
and talk. I wrote you a long letter some two weeks since
and a long one to John. I added a postscript to each and
sent them by the first construction train that left
here to repair the road, in care of Capt Hart of our
Regiment, who was captured at Chickamauga and recently escaped from Columbia, S. C. I hear to-day that
train was captured if so the letters are gone. And Oh
how hard for poor Capt. Hart. I hope it is not true
but fear it is. The letter was an important one, for in it
I bid you prepare to be ready to come back with me if
I come back, and the one to John was a business one.
Well I will know soon and if they are gone I must
write them over again. My time of departure is very

uncertain now I cannot leave till this campaign is over and Genl Thomas comes back here, it may be a month or two yet. As before stated my visit home will determine whether I stay in the army or not, and if I do I shall want you to come with me. I have two rooms and a kitchen selected for us, very rough to be sure but it will be a home. It is pretty well decided that Hd Quarters will be here for some time, and if I should be ordered to my Regiment it is only on Lookout Mountain, so we might as well seize the opportunity, the first of the war, and be together while we can. And if by any chance I do not get home, which disaster I do not foresee at all, I can send for you to come here. So be ready for anything dearest. . . . The war news is very encouraging all round and another year I hope will end this war. How our "Old Tom" has done things, how proud we all are of him. I have a despatch from him this morning telling me to stay where I am, as Hd Quarters will be reestablished here very soon, so address me as usual. Oh it was so good to get your letters but I hope next mail will bring later ones. . . . Well Good bye I hope you are having a happy Christmas and will have a happy New Year. I wish I could get something to the children with love to all and the compliments of the season I am as ever your true husband

Alfred

OFFICE ASSISTANT
COMMISSARY OF MUSTERS,
District of Tennessee,
Nashville, Tenn., Jan 5th 1865

Dearest Mary,

Here I am in Nashville most unexpectedly. I came here to meet the General on business and the interview has knocked all my calculations on the head. The General has pushed what is left of Hood's Army across the Tennessee River, and has come back here himself to arrange matters for another campaign, he returns to the front day after tomorrow, and tomorrow will decide whether I go with him or remain here, as the campaign will be towards Corinth, and I must either be with him or on the line of communication between the army and Washington, tomorrow will decide it. If I go with him of course my visit home will be at an end for the present.[5] If I remain here I can get off pretty soon. So wait till my next letter for a decision; at all events it don't look much like my bringing you back with me. I write in great haste and am weary having travelled all night. . . . With all love to you and ours as ever yours

Alfred

Nashville Sunday Feb 12/65

My Dearest Mary

I arrived here safely last night having missed every connection again on the route. . . . My arrival was very opportune Genl Thomas having reached here only an hour before me, and had business for me this morning. I have just left him. I find myself plunged into an abyss of work. The Dept of the Ohio is merged into the Dept of the Cumberland, and all the work of this Dept

[5] Hough's long-anticipated leave came to him in January of 1865. As he relates the events, "We had a train through on the 2nd of January 65 bringing with it an order for me to join the General [Thomas] at Nashville at once, and on the 4th I was with him and found urgent and important business for me. [Plans for a new campaign.] This was soon completed and then my long wish for leave was given and I started for Lewisburg, Pa. to my family where there was another happy reunion. My leave was for one month but before it had expired I received a despatch to return to Nashville immediately. It was hard to leave, but orders are orders, and on the 11th of February I was again in Nashville."

has now to be reorganized by me their system having been different from mine, I am to relieve Capt Paxton Mustering & Disbursing Officer for the State of Tennessee and investigate his old business and make a report, misconduct having been charged against him (this is private) but the order says "This order will not be construed as relieving Capt Hough of his duties as Chf Com Musters Dept of Cumberland". So you see I have much additional labor put upon me and a great deal of it new business, which I have to educate myself to, but I shall go at it with a will. The order from War Dept is looked upon as a great compliment to me by all here, and Genl Thomas has also shown his confidence in me by retaining me as Chf C M Dept of Cumberland as the Chf C M Dept of Ohio is a Lt Col of the Regular Army, and an old acquaintance of the General's. He however relieves him and retains me. I had a long and satisfactory talk with him this morning. All this secures my residence in Nashville, for some time at least, and you can commence to put your house in order to join me. I have not yet relieved Capt Paxton he being absent, I have also got to remove my office from Chattanooga, which I am giving the orders for to-day. I suppose I shall get Capt Paxton's quarters, but I don't know how good they are I shall however immediately on his return which will be on Wednesday decide upon what to do, and then can say whether you are to board or keep house and when I want you to come, but with the little information I have I think you can come as soon as you can get ready say two or three weeks, any how before the 1st of April. . . . This is all I can say to-day, as I have work before me which will take every moment of my time for days to come. . . . your loving husband

Alfred

Nashville Feb 26th 1865

My Dearest Mary

. . . By this time I hope you have my letters telling you to come on here and are out of suspense. I am to have possession of the house *possibly* on the 1st of April and before that if *possible* so I want you to come on just as soon as you choose and can get ready and by the time you have made a visit at Indianapolis and get here it will be nearly up to the time, and if you get here before the house is vacant we can live at a hotel till it is ready. So come as soon as you can and let me know at once the time you fix so that I can make arrangements to meet or send for you at Louisville.

I will describe your future temporary home the best I can. It will not contrast well [with] Claude Melnotte's description to Pauline of her home on the banks of the lake of Como but still it will do for a home. The house is an old frame formerly occupied by a Methodist minister who has gone "secesh". It is just on a boundary line between two fashionable parts of the city, but the ground just there being low the neighborhood is not all built upon and the vacant ground is strewed with carts and other Govt material, but we have a brown stone house right next door and one square's walk brings you to the fashionable street (as was). There are two large rooms down stairs and two up, with a hall between a portico on the whole front both on 1st and second story one which opens into from one of the large rooms just the place for us and the children. There are back buildings separated from the house where negroes live so we can't use them except to put our own in, everything looks very desolate and dirty around the house and in the yard but that can be fixed. Capt Paxton occupies the house in this way—one of the rooms down stairs is the office the other the parlor one up stairs is kitchen and dining room and the other the sleeping room. I propose to move the office elsewhere and use that for a kitchen and the parlor for a dining and sitting room leaving us the two rooms up stairs for chambers. The house is carpeted (very old) plenty of heavy furniture, bed steads bureaus wardrobes and some chairs and sofas and two mattresses. We can buy a cooking stove and utensils here, and to complete our outfit we want bedding, pillows, and table furniture, which you must pack up and send to me by express. You must bring *with you only two trunks and a hat box at most.* The other things needed that these will not hold you must pack up as I said, mark to me at Hd Quarters Dept of Cumb. Nashville and send by express make it as small as possible as the freight will be high and I expect you will have to prepay it. Be sure and bring my tin box. . . . Your easiest trip will be to leave Louisburg [Lewisburg] in the morning get to Harrisburg about 1 P.M. leave there at 4.15 get to Pittsburgh about 2 in the morning change cars there and get to Crestline about noon next day change again and get to Indianapolis about 9½ at night where you must have somebody to meet you. I recommend this schedule because it is easier to change cars at night at Pittsburgh than at Crestline. If you make the connections it will be all right but if you do not you must figure it out the best you can. You had better send the things that are to come by express at once as I can store them in my office till we get the house. I am hard at work, and will be for some time. With love to all I am your true husband

Alfred

*   *   *   *   *   *   *   *   *

With Captain Hough's letter of February 26, which made final arrangements for his wife to join him, the correspondence comes to a close. From then until the war's end he remained at Nashville, working for Thomas. It was in this year that an event occurred which was to keep him in the army the rest of his life. "The General losing all his Volunteer Staff Officers by the gradual discharge taking place, now appointed me Acting Assistant Adjt. General, and with these duties upon me the year 1865 kept me busily occupied; in fact at no period of my life have I labored more assiduously and continually than I did at this time, from early morning till late at night I was kept at the desk." Despite his complaint about the hard work, Hough was flattered by the appointment and very shortly thereafter he was given the position of Aide de Camp to Thomas, a position he retained until the General's death in 1870.

BIBLIOGRAPHY

* * * * * * * * *

Blegen, Theodore C. (ed.), *The Civil War Letters of Colonel Hans Christian Heg*, Northfield, Minnesota, 1936.

Bowman, Colonel S. M. and Irwin, Lt. Col. R. B., *Sherman and His Campaigns: A Military Biography*, New York, 1865.

Cleaves, Freeman, *Rock of Chickamauga: The Life of General George H. Thomas*, Norman, Oklahoma, 1948.

Grant, U. S., *Personal Memoirs of U. S. Grant*, Two volumes, New York, 1885.

Hight, John J., *History of the Fifty Eighth Regiment of Indiana Volunteer Infantry*, Princeton, Indiana, 1895.

Horn, Stanley F., *The Army of Tennessee, A Military History*, New York, 1941.

Johnston, Joseph E., *Narrative of Military Operations Directed During the Late War Between the States by Joseph E. Johnston*, New York, 1874.

Leech, Margaret, *Reveille in Washington, 1860-1865*, New York, 1941.

Moore, Frank (ed.), *The Rebellion Record*, Eleven volumes, New York, 1862-1868.

Van Horne, Thomas B., *The Life of Major General George H. Thomas*, New York, 1882.

Wiley, Bell Irvin, *The Life of Billy Yank: The Common Soldier of the Union*, Indianapolis and New York, 1952.

Winther, Oscar Osburn (ed.), *With Sherman to the Sea: The Civil War Letters, Diaries & Reminiscences of Theodore F. Upson*, Baton Rouge, Louisiana, 1943.

OFFICIAL RECORDS

The War of the Rebellion: A Compilation of the Official Records of the Union and Confederate Armies, Seventy vols., Washington, 1880-1901.
Official Army Register, 1863.

ARTICLES

Athearn, Robert G. (ed.), "An Indiana Doctor Marches with Sherman: The Diary of James Comfort Patten," *Indiana Magazine of History,* XLIX, No. 4, December, 1953, 405-423.

Barnhart, John D., "A Hoosier Invades the Confederacy: Letters and Diaries of Leroy S. Mayfield," *Indiana Magazine of History,* XXXIX, No. 2, June, 1943, 144-192.

Harwell, Richard B. (ed.), "The Campaign from Chattanooga to Atlanta as seen by a Federal Soldier," *The Georgia Historical Quarterly,* XXV, No. 3, September, 1941, 262-279.

Hay, Thomas R., "The Atlanta Campaign," *The Georgia Historical Quarterly,* VII, No. 1, March, 1923, 19-44; VII, No. 2, June, 1923, 100-119.

"Letters of a Badger Boy in Blue: The Atlanta Campaign," Chauncey H. Cooke. *The Wisconsin Magazine of History,* V, 1921-22, 63-99. The earlier Cooke letters appear in Volume IV, but are not pertinent to this work.

Osborn, George C. (ed.), "Civil War Letters of Robert W. Banks: Atlanta Campaign," *The Georgia Historical Quarterly,* XXVII, No. 2, June, 1943, 208-217.

Perkerson, Medora Field (ed.), "A Civil War Letter on the Capture of Atlanta," *The Georgia Historical Quarterly,* XXVIII, No. 4, December, 1944, 251-270.

Padgett, James A. (ed.), "With Sherman Through Georgia and the Carolinas: Letters of a Federal Soldier," *The Georgia Historical Quarterly,* XXXII, No. 4, December, 1948, 284-323; XXXIII, No. 1, March, 1949, 49-81.

"War Diary of Thaddeus H. Capron, 1861-1865," *Journal of the Illinois State Historical Society,* XII, No. 3, October, 1919, 330-407.

INDEX

Date Due